AN

# ELEMENTARY COURSE

OF

# MILITARY ENGINEERING.

## PART II.

## PERMANENT FORTIFICATIONS.

BY

D. H. MAHAN, LL.D.,

PROFESSOR OF MILITARY AND CIVIL ENGINEERING IN THE UNITED STATES MILITARY ACADEMY.

---

NEW YORK:
JOHN WILEY & SON, 535 BROADWAY.
1867.

THE NEW YORK PRINTING COMPANY,
81, 83, *and* 85 *Centre Street*,
NEW YORK

# PREFACE.

THE contents of this volume were not intended for publication in their present form; having been arranged specially with regard to the limited time allowed, for instruction in this branch of their studies, to the Cadets of the United States Military Academy.

In this arrangement, the chief object had in view has been to enable the pupil to examine intelligently the productions of others, and to present his own ideas understandingly. To effect this, the attempt has been made to give, in as concise a form as practicable, the general principles of Permanent Fortification, and their applications, as presented in the writings and practice of military engineers whose works are accepted as professional standards.

Particular prominence has been given to Noizet's Method as an instructive elementary exercise; both as to the manner of combining the elements of a bastioned front, and of delineating with accuracy its various details.

# ELEMENTS

OF

# PERMANENT FORTIFICATION.

## CHAPTER I.

### PRELIMINARY CONSIDERATIONS AND COMPONENT ELEMENTS OF PERMANENT DEFENCES.

SUMMARY.

Permanent fortification, its objects and means of attainment (Art. 1).—Description and analysis of the usual general profile (Art. 5).—Description of recent modified profile (Art. 8).—Command (Art. 9).—Description and discussion of scarps (Art. 10).—Counterscarps (Art. 11).—Ditch (Art. 12).—Face covers (Art. 13).—General remarks on the general profile (Art. 14).—Classes of open defences (Art. 15).—Loop-holed walls (Art. 16).—Exterior corridors (Art. 17).—Barbette batteries (Art. 18).—Embrasure batteries (Art. 19).—Machicouli defences (Art. 20).—Detached scarp walls (Art. 21).—Semi-detached scarp walls (Art. 22).—Scarp galleries (Art. 23).—Counterscarp galleries (Art. 24).—Bastionnets (Art. 25).—Caponnière defences for enceinte ditch (Art. 26).—General Remarks (Art. 27).—Casemates on land fronts (Art. 28).—Mortar casemates (Art. 29).—Casemates for water fronts (Art. 30).—Embrasures of casemates (Art. 31).—Bomb-proof buildings (Art. 32).—Powder magazines (Art. 33).—General remarks on communications (Art. 34).—Particular conditions that communications should satisfy (Art. 35).—Ramps (Art. 36).—Stairs (Art. 37).—Posterns (Art. 38)—Gateway (Art. 39).—Port-Cullis (Art. 40).—Classes of enceintes (Art. 41).—Systems and methods of fortification (Art. 42).—General remarks (Art. 43).—General remarks on outworks (Art. 44).—General conditions outworks should satisfy (Art. 45).—Classes of outworks (Art. 46).—Covered-way (Art. 47).—Places of arms (Art. 48).—Traverses (Art. 49)—Tenaille (Art. 50).—Demi-lune (Art. 51).—Counterguard (Art. 52).—Redoubts (Art. 53).—Tenaillon (Art. 54).—Horn-work (Art. 55).—Crown-work (Art. 56).—Advanced and detached works (Art. 57).—Interior retrenchments and cavaliers (Art. 60).

## I.

### PRELIMINARY CONSIDERATIONS.

**1.** THE term *permanent fortification* is applied to those defences which, constructed of materials of a durable nature, and designed for permanent occupancy by troops, receive such a degree of strength that an enemy will be forced to the operations either of a siege or a blockade, to gain possession of them.

**2.** These defences differ from temporary fortification but in degree; the general principles of defensive works being alike applicable to both.

**3.** The object of such defences is to secure the permanent military possession of those points, either on the frontiers, or in the interior of a state, which must, at all times, have a well defined bearing on the operations of a defensive or an offensive war.

**4.** For the attainment of this object, the following general conditions should be fulfilled in the arrangement of such defences:

1st. *They should be of sufficient strength to resist with success all the ordinary means resorted to by an assailant in an open assault.*

2d. *Be provided with suitable shelters to protect the troops, the armament, and the magazines of provisions and munitions of war required for their defence against the destructive measures of the assailant of every description.*

3d. *Be so planned that every point exterior to the defences within cannon range shall be thoroughly swept by their fire.*

4th. *Have secure and easy means of communication for the movements of the troops, both within the defences and to the exterior.*

5th. *And, finally, be provided with all such accessory defensive means as the natural features of the position itself may afford, to enable the garrison to dispute with energy the occupancy by the assailant of every point both within and exterior to the defences.*

The defensive branch of the military engineer's art consists in a knowledge of the means which are employed to fulfil the above conditions, and of their suitable adaptation to the natural features of the positions he may be called upon to fortify.

## II.

### COMPONENT ELEMENTS OF PERMANENT WORKS.

#### GENERAL PROFILE.

**5.** The first condition laid down for permanent defences, security from open assault, supposes a strength of profile greatly superior to that which is given to temporary works.

6. The usual and most simple form of profile for permanent works consists of a *rampart;* a *parapet;* and a *ditch*, the *scarp* and *counterscarp* of which are faced with *steep walls* of *stone* or *brick*, and exterior to which a *glacis* is usually thrown up.

When the ditch contains at all times a depth of water sufficient to prevent its being forded, the scarp and counterscarp may be simply slopes of earth like those of field works; as the water, with ordinary vigilance on the part of the defence, will give security from surprise, and all the other ordinary means of an open assault.

**The Rampart,** A, Pl. 3, Figs. 4, 6, is an earthen mound, raised above the natural level of the ground, and upon which the parapet B is placed.

The rampart thus serves to give the troops and armament, which are placed on top of it and behind the parapet, a commanding view over the ground to be guarded by the fire of the defences; whilst, at the same time, it increases the obstacle to an open assault, by the additional height it gives to the scarp.

The top surface of the rampart, b c, in rear of the parapet, termed the *terre-plein*, affords the troops and armament a convenient position for circulation from point to point, where they are sheltered from the direct views of the assailants' fire.

The rampart is usually terminated on the interior, a b, by allowing the earth to assume either its natural slope, or one somewhat less steep, and which is termed the *rampart-slope.*

In cases where this slope would take up too much of the ground within the defences it is replaced by a wall, termed the *parade-wall*, which rises from the level of the interior gound, termed the *parade*, to the interior line of the *terre-plein.*

Inclined planes of earth, termed *ramps*, lead from the parade to the terre-plein, being placed against the rampart-slope, or the parade-wall. The ramps are, in some cases, terminated, inwardly, with the same slope as that of the rampart; in othe s, this slope is replaced by a wall, which rises to the top surface of the ramp, or a little above it.

7. **The Parapet,** serving the same purposes in permanent as in field works, receives the same general form as in the latter.

In some cases the exterior slope, Pl. 3, Fig. 12, is replaced by a wall, which, resting on the top of the scarp wall, rises to the level of the superior slope.

The exterior slope of the parapet usually rises from the top of the scarp wall, leaving a narrow berm between it and the scarp, or face of the wall.

In some cases, however, it is thrown so far to the rear of the scarp, Pl. 3, Figs. 9, 10, as to leave sufficient room for a communication C, in front of the parapet, in which the troops can circulate under cover from fire, being masked either by an earthen parapet, or by a wall, D. This covered communication, C, is termed an *exterior corridor* or *chemin-de-rondes.*

The essential properties of the parapet, as in field works, are to afford cover from the enemy's missiles, and every facility for sweeping his positions by the fire of its artillery and small-arms.

To afford cover against the heaviest guns that can now be brought to bear with effect against a parapet, a thickness of 27 feet for ordinary earth, and of 23 feet when either pure sand or a soil with a large proportion of sand is used, would, from the more recent experiments on the penetration of projectiles, seem to be amply sufficient. The most of the parapets of existing works have received only from 18 to 20 feet, and these will doubtless be found to give efficient cover against any ordinary attack.

In small works of less importance and not liable to be breached, the thickness may be reduced to 12 or 15 feet.

For the superior slope, the rule, so long in use, of making it six base to one perpendicular, or $\frac{1}{6}$, is still generally followed.

This rule has not been adopted because cannon cannot be fired under a greater depression than $\frac{1}{6}$, although from the inconveniences attending greater depressions than this, artillerists are unwilling to resort to them; but from a greater depression necessitating the employment of very deep embrasures, or else that of platforms raised so high to the rear, that the men serving the guns will be very much exposed to fire.

Still, where a greater or less plunge is necessary, to bring the exterior ground better under fire, it should be adopted; as it is to be observed, that the strength of the parapet, at the angle of the interior crest, should be increased where the assailant can have a plunging fire on it; whereas, when exposed to a fire from a level much below this crest, the angle at it will be less exposed, and the plunge of the parapet can be increased without injury.

Until within a recent period, the interior slope, the banquette and banquette slope received the same forms and dimensions as in field works; the top of the rampart falling, from the foot of the banquette slope to the crest of the rampart slope, one foot, to drain off the surface-water.

8. At present, the profile most generally adopted for this part of the parapet and rampart is the one shown in Pl. 3, Fig. 4, in which the portion of the top of the rampart for a distance of 15 feet back from the interior crest is held on a level of $6\frac{3}{4}$ feet below the interior crest, and serves as a general barbette for heavy guns; whilst the remaining portion of the top surface is placed at a level of 8 feet below the interior crest, and made wide enough to serve as a roadway in rear of the general barbette; the two levels being connected by a slope of $\frac{1}{1}$ or $\frac{1}{2}$; and the roadway receiving a slight pitch to the rear for drainage.

In the older works, the terre-plein received a breadth of from 40 to 50 feet, estimated between the interior crest and the exterior line of the terre-plein. For motives of economy, and sometimes to enlarge the parade, this breadth was reduced to 20 or 24 feet, and a parade wall substituted for the rampart slope.

In the later profile, the interior slope is $\frac{1}{1}$, and has a banquette tread of only 2 feet, with a banquette slope of only $\frac{1}{1}$. Where guns are mounted either in barbette or embrasure, the interior slope is increased to $\frac{3}{1}$, and the banquette and its slope removed; the earth taken off by these modifications serving to form the merlons between the shallow embrasures cut into the parapets.

When the foot of the exterior slope rests on the top of the scarp wall, a berm of 2 feet in breadth is left between it and the edge of the coping. This breadth of berm is objectionable, as giving a good landing-place for a scaling party in an open assault; and it is proposed, when the work is in danger of an attack, to reduce the berm to 18 inches or one foot, by increasing the thickness of the parapet 6 inches or one foot.

The exterior slope, for the reasons given in discussing the parapets of field works, should not be less, on land fronts, than the natural slope of the earth of which the parapet is formed. In sea-coast works, where the parapet is high, and can be reached, within cannon range, only by elevating the guns of the ships, the exterior slope may be replaced by a vertical revetment of stone, or one of sods with but a slight inclination, as, from the direction of the fire, this facing, even if partially destroyed, will not cause such weakness in the parapet as to expose the troops. By using a facing of this kind the parapet will occupy less room and leave more interior space, which in small works is often desirable.

**9.** The *command*, or height of the parapet above the site, has a very important bearing in the defence of permanent works.

In the first place, the greater the command, the greater will be the plunge of the guns on the exterior ground, and the more difficulty will the assailant meet with in obtaining cover in his trenches from this plunge; being obliged to make them deeper than usual, and to increase the height of their parapets.

In the second place, having to fire under greater angles of elevation, as the command is greater, the plunge of his shot, when his enfilading batteries are brought near the work, becomes so great that the balls will not ricochet, and the effects of his fire will thus be lessened.

Motives of economy, however, require the command to be restricted within quite narrow limits. When the work consists of a simple enceinte enveloped by a covered way, the command may be reduced to 16 feet; allowing a command of 8 feet to the interior crest of the glacis over the site, and a height of 8 feet to the interior crest above the coping, which, with the rest of the scarp wall, to be masked by the glacis, must not rise above the level of its interior crest. When there are other outworks besides the covered way in defensive relations with the enceinte, the latter cannot receive a command over the site of less than 20 feet, in order to give it a suitable command over the whole of the outworks.

**10. Scarp.** A scarp wall 30 feet high is usually admitted as a sufficient protection in dry ditches against an escalade.

This rule, drawn from the experience of sieges, and the opinions of the most eminent engineers, seems a safe one; since to scale a wall of this height would require ladders of sufficient length to enable the men who ascend to step from the ladder, when planted securely against the wall, on the coping, and of sufficient strength to bear the weight of six or eight men mounting together.

To carry forward ladders of the dimensions requisite for

this purpose and place them in position, with that promptitude upon which the success of an open assault must mainly depend, would of itself be an operation of no slight difficulty; but when it is considered that the assailants are exposed to the fire of the defences before reaching the ditch, which from its width and depth alone renders it a serious obstacle, and that after they have entered the ditch they are still under the fire by which it is flanked, it is difficult to imagine how the attempt could succeed if the assailed offered even an ordinary degree of resistance.

The above heights of scarp walls rest, as has been stated, upon the practice of the most eminent engineers, and are founded on the experience of assaults by scaling.

There are among engineers partisans for scarps of greater heights than these averages, who base their opinions upon the facts that scarps of 40 feet have been successfully scaled, and that very light and strong scaling ladders, formed of several separate pieces, which can be promptly put together and raised with ease, have been successfully tried; whilst others, basing their opinions upon the many bloody repulses of open assaults made upon field works of only an ordinary profile, are in favor of low or medium scarps of from 12 to 16 feet high.

That scarps over 30 feet high have been scaled is true; but the success was owing to a want of ordinary precautions on the part of the assailed, and to the garrison not being of suitable strength to guard all points efficiently.

That heavy assaults upon comparatively weak field-works have been repulsed with great slaughter, we have also plentiful records of in our own and European contests. But in these cases, the numerical strength of the contending parties under fire was nearly equal, and the defence of the most vigorous character, so that any shelter, however slight, would have inclined the balance on the side of the assailed.

These are extreme cases, upon which it would be very unsound to base rules for practice. As the object of all fortifications is to supply the place of numerical weakness on the part of the defence, the safer practice would seem to be to do this by placing such an obstacle in the way of an open assault that but a few men, promptly availing themselves of it, might frustrate long enough the attempt of the assailant to give time to gather sufficient force at the point assailed to render the attack abortive.

Besides securing the place from an escalade, scarp walls

act as retaining walls, to hold up the excavated side of the ditch towards the rampart, the rampart itself, and the parapet. This requires that they should receive a thickness and form of profile adapted to this end.

The top stone of the wall, k, termed the *cordon*, or *coping*, projects beyond its face, and, serving as a *larmier* or *drip*, protects it from the effects of the rain water, which runs from the parapet upon the coping.

The line in which the face of the scarp wall if prolonged would intersect the coping is termed the *magistral*. This is a very important line in drawing the plans of permanent works, serving as the directing line to fix, both upon the drawing and upon the ground in setting out the work, the dimensions and relative positions of all the bounding lines of the parapet and other parts.

Although no ordinary scarp walls can resist breaching, and have to be covered by earthen masks to screen them from the distant fire of the assailed, they should be so constructed as to render breaching a difficult operation ; limiting the breach made to the part of the wall actually destroyed by the assailant's projectiles.

In the scarp walls of Vauban and Cormontaigne, and in many of the more modern fortifications of Europe, the scarp walls are built solid, with counterforts on their back, of the forms and dimensions adopted by Vauban. This engineer gave his scarps a batir of $\frac{5}{1}$. Cormontaigne, finding that the faces of these walls were soon injured by the weather, adopted a batir of $\frac{6}{1}$. This for the same reason was increased by some to $\frac{12}{1}$, by others to $\frac{20}{1}$ ; and, in our climate, where the action of the weather on masonry is very injurious, our engineers have varied their batir from $\frac{24}{1}$ to $\frac{48}{1}$.

To give greater efficacy to the resistance offered to breaching, and to prevent the breach from taking a gentle slope when formed, it has been proposed by some to back the wall and counterforts by a kind of pisé work, or with beton with but little lime in it, of several feet in thickness.

Others have proposed, for the same purpose, to connect the end of the counterforts by vertical arches, and to fill the cells thus formed either with pisé, or with this poor beton.

Others prefer long thin counterforts sustaining several tiers of relieving arches; the cells thus formed being left open for defence, for bomb-proof shelters, and for magazines for provisions, &c.

All these expedients have been tried, though not fully

tested, by experiment; the last, under all points of view, having the most advantages in its favor.

Among the variety of scarp walls proposed, the *detached* and *semi-detached* have each their partisans.

In the former, the back of the wall rises from the bottom of the ditch, leaving, between it and the foot of the rampart behind it, a breadth of several feet, either on the same level as the bottom of the ditch, or raised a few feet above this level. In some cases, the wall is built with several tiers of arched recesses on its back; the portions of the wall in front of which are pierced with loop-holes; each recess being of sufficient size to give shelter to several men serving the loop-holes, and firing into the ditch, or on the top of the counterscarp.

In the latter, the lower portion of the wall is built with relieving arches, either closed or open in rear; the upper portion, for a height from 8 to 12 feet, being detached from the rampart and prepared for defence like the preceding example.

Scarp walls of this character have some advantages over the non-detached. They offer the same obstacle to an escalade as the latter; and, when the assailant has gained the top of the wall, they present the further difficulty of his getting down on the other side. They give a good fire upon the ditch, and are thus favorable to the safety of sortie parties in retreat. And, when a wide space is left between them and the parapet, room is afforded for the formation of a column on each side of any breach made in the wall, to charge an assaulting column entering the breach in flank.

On the other hand, these walls favor an assaulting column rushing through a breach in them; as the assailants can spread along the corridor on the right and left, and assault the work on a wider front. Should the assailant not choose this course, he has the alternative of establishing himself securely upon the exterior slope in trenches; and if it suits his purposes better, to drive a mine gallery from the breach into the rampart, to blow it up and open a breach into the work.

But a very glaring defect in all of these detached scarps is the exposed condition in which the men behind them are from the splinters from the walls, when the corridor can be enfiladed; and from the splinters of exploding shells, which either lodge and explode in the rampart, or roll down it and explode in the corridor.

To break in some measure the effects of this enfilade, and also to prevent an assaulting column from spreading to the right and left along the corridor, traverse walls, having doors in them for communication and loop-holed to fire along the corridor, are placed from point to point, running from the scarp wall back to the rampart slope across the corridor. But these cross walls would soon be destroyed by an ordinary enfilade, and the splinters from them would render the corridor untenable.

**11. Counterscarp Wall.** A revetted counterscarp is regarded as adding to the difficulty of descending into the ditch, and as offering greater security against an open assault. For this purpose the wall should not be less than 12 or 15 feet in height to offer a serious impediment; in any case, where motives of economy do not imperiously demand it, the counterscarp wall of the enceinte should be from 18 to 24 feet in height. This height will not only give great security to the ditch, but, as will be seen in the description of the siege works of the assailant, it will delay considerably his progress, as the gallery by which he must generally reach the bottom of the ditch from the level of the covered-way terre-plein is one of the slowest and most laborious of his operations.

Besides giving greater security against a surprise, a revetted counterscarp enables the assailed to circulate through their ditches even when the assailant has established his trenches along the glacis crest, as the top of the counterscarp wall will screen the troops passing along the bottom of the ditch.

It also affords facilities for forming a counterscarp gallery behind it loopholed for the defence of the ditch in an open assault, which, for small works without thorough flanking arrangements, will be found very serviceable.

Besides, this gallery will be found of great utility where a system of defensive mines is to form a part of the defences.

But as counterscarp galleries, if seized upon by the assailant, may be turned against the defences, it is important that they should be placed in positions where they will be of little value to the assailant if seized upon.

The necessity for revetting with a wall of masonry the scarp and counterscarp of a wet ditch in which the water can be retained at a level of six feet in depth, is not so obvious; as when the ditch is wide the obstacle of the water alone would seem to be sufficient to secure the place from a surprise. Many works under this condition have been built with simple earthen scarps and counterscarps; in some instances a chemin-de-ronde being formed by leaving a wide berm between the foot of the exterior slope and the crest of the scarp, and planting a loop-holed stockade near the crest.

But in rigorous climates, where the water freezes hard, a wet ditch is no longer a security in winter; and a revetted scarp of at least 24 feet in height, with a steep earthen counterscarp, is a better security against a surprise than the expedients proposed, of keeping an open channel along the middle of the ditch of 12 feet in width; piling up on each side of it the ice taken from the channel; and throwing water over the exterior slopes to freeze and form a slippery surface to an assaulting column.

**12. Ditch.** The width and depth of the enceinte ditch depend mainly upon the amount of embankment required for the enceinte and the glacis, and therefore will result from the calculation for equalizing the excavation and embankment which these demand.

A deep and narrow ditch offers the advantage of presenting more difficulty to the assailant in reaching the bottom of it, either in an open assault, or by a gallery in the attack by regular approaches, thus prolonging the defence.

It masks better the sally-ports from the enemy's fire by allowing them to be placed so low that the projectiles coming over the counterscarp cannot reach them.

In like manner by drawing in the crest of the glacis nearer to the scarp the latter will be better masked by it from the plunge of the distant fire of the assailant's batteries; and cannot be breached so low down from his batteries placed along the glacis crest.

On the other hand, when the ditch is narrow and deep it may be partly filled by breaching the scarp, and then blowing in the counterscarp so as by the united *débris* to form an easy roadway for an assaulting column to enter the work.

A wide ditch, on the other hand, requires more labor to construct the trench across it by which the assailant can reach the foot of the breach under cover. This is a consideration of some importance in wet ditches, where the assailant is obliged to construct a dike upon which the parapet of his cover is placed.

In the practice of engineers the enceinte ditch has received a width of from 20 to 30 yards when dry, and from

30 to 45 yards when wet. These dimensions may be reduced to within 10 or 12 yards where the embankments are not great and circumstances are unfavorable to an attempt at escalade.

The bottom of the ditch, when dry, usually receives a slight slope from the foot of the scarp and counterscarp to its centre, where a small drain, termed a *cunette*, is dug to receive the surface water and keep the ditch dry. In some cases, from motives of economy, the difference of level between the cunette and the foot of the counterscarp wall is increased, thus giving a less height of wall. This practice, however, can only be followed where the foundations of the wall will be secure, from the soil of the bottom of the ditch being of such a nature as not to yield from the effects of the weather upon it.

**13. Face Covers.** Engineers since the times of Cormontaigne have mostly adopted his method of placing the top of the scarp wall on a level with the crest of the glacis, or a little below this crest, to give the wall cover from the assailant's distant batteries. But this is evidently only a partial remedy, since the plunge of projectiles fired from a distance is very great in the descending branch of the trajectory, and with the rifled guns now used, these projectiles fired from a distance may pass over the glacis crest and strike the wall quite low down, thus effecting serious damage; particularly in the case of wide and shallow ditches.

Various expedients have been proposed by engineers to remedy this defect. Choumara, an engineer of celebrity, has proposed to form what he terms an interior glacis within the ditch, the crest of which shall rise so high above the bottom of the ditch, that it shall mask the scarp wall from the plunge of the distant batteries, and shall force the assailant to establish his breaching batteries on this interior glacis to enable him to fire low enough to effect a practicable breach in the wall.

Brialmont, a more recent writer, proposes a like plan for the same purposes; and in one of our own works, Fort Warren, Boston Harbor, a heavy earthen face cover masks a portion of the scarp wall, from a position from which a breaching fire might have been brought against the part thus masked.

**14. General Remarks.** The command of the parapet over the exterior ground and any outworks of the defences, its *relief*, or height above the bottom of the ditch, and its height above the top of the scarp wall, are all points which call for a careful consideration on the part of the engineer in any combination of these that he may be called upon to make.

First, it is important that the parapet should thoroughly sweep all the ground within range of its guns, at least up to the glacis crest; and the more so as the closer the assailant's trenches approach the work, the greater will be the plunge obtained upon them, and the more difficult it will be for the assailant to cover himself by his trenches.

That the parapet should command all outworks within range of its fire is obvious, otherwise when seized upon by the assailant these outworks would have a plunging fire upon the main work.

The rule is laid down by some authorities, that the projectiles of the parapet should clear the crest of the glacis by at least 2 feet. But this is by no means necessary, for if the glacis has a covered way for troops in its rear, it will be inpracticable to keep these troops in the covered way with missiles passing in such close proximity to them, particularly as they are subjected to annoyance from the wads, and may sustain occasional losses from awkward cannoneers, and the bursting of shells in their rear.

The relief of the parapet of the flanking parts of the work should evidently be such that every point along the foot of the scarp wall shall be swept by its fire. This supposes also a certain correlation between the relief and the length of the lines flanked, so that this condition shall be satisfied; a relation that can always be easily found, either by calculation, or a very simple geometrical construction from given *data*.

In like manner the height of the interior crest of the parapet above the top of the scarp wall, can be easily ascertained by the same methods, with assumed *data*. It should evidently be at least such that a gun, on any kind of carriage, firing through an embrasure of assumed depth, and under a given depression, shall clear the coping of the wall about one foot.

A mere geometrical diagram will show that as the height of the interior crest above the top of the wall, supposing the position of the latter fixed, is increased, the whole parapet will be thrown further back from the wall, and the interior space of the work will be in the same degree lessened.

All of these considerations therefore suggest that nothing like absolute rules can be laid down so as to give a routine character to the practice of this branch of the military art.

The rules here given with respect to the form and dimensions of the general profile of the enceinte are founded upon reasons growing out of the nature of the question, and as such have served as guides to engineers in the practice of their profession. As they have stood besides the test of long experience, it is safe to follow them, whilst at the same time the engineer should not hesitate to vary from them when satisfied, after careful examination, that the case before him requires it. Fortification, it must be remembered, is like all other arts. It has its canons, which are founded upon the nature of the question, and its rules of practice based upon these and upon experience. As the latter presents to the engineer new facts, his practice must be made to conform to them; but the general principles of his art must ever remain the same, and be his invariable guide.

## III.

### OPEN DEFENCES.

**15.** By this term are understood the dispositions made for the action of the troops and armament which are covered from the missiles of the assailed by the parapet alone.

To this class belong the arrangement of the parapet which has already been described; simple *loop-holed walls* for musketry used as inclosures of gorges, &c.; *exterior corridors* which are covered either by a wall or an earthen parapet; and *barbettes and embrasures* for artillery.

**16. Loop-Holed Walls.** Walls of this class, when used as the inclosures of the gorges of lunettes or other isolated works, placed in advance of the enceinte, but within the reach of its artillery fire, should be high enough to secure the work from an open assault, and sufficiently thick to resist the occasional shot which may reach them over the parapet by which they are covered. For these purposes the height, Pl. 4, Fig. 24, should be from 12 to 15 feet, and the thickness from 4 to 5 feet. The loop-holes are not placed nearer to each other than from 3 to 4 feet, estimated between their axes. They should be at least 6 feet above the exterior foot of the wall, and 4¼ feet above the ground or banquette within. The loop-holes are usually placed at regular intervals along the line of the wall; or only opposite that portion of the exterior ground upon which a fire is to be brought to bear.

The form and dimensions of the loop-hole will depend upon the thickness of the wall and the field of view, both vertically and horizontally, which is to be covered by its fire. The plan is either trapezoidal, Pl. 4, Figs. 17, 20, widening from the front of the wall inwards, or else it widens from the centre each way to the front and back; or, as is the more usual form in our works, the interior portion from the centre widens inwards, whilst the exterior part is rectangular in plan, and of the same width as the width on the interior or back of the wall. The first form is best adapted to walls not more than 2½ feet thick, the others to heavier walls; the object being to lessen, as far as practicable, the weakness which loop-holes necessarily cause to the wall; this defect increasing as the exterior or interior opening is greater.

For thin walls, where the plan of the loop-hole is trapezoidal, the width of the exterior opening may be from 2 to 4 inches, and that of the interior from 15 to 18 inches. These dimensions, however, may vary according to the field of fire to be brought within the range of the loop-hole, the more or less cover to be given to the troops, and the strength of the masonry of which the wall is formed. The vertical dimensions of the loop-hole, both on the interior and the exterior, will depend upon the field of fire to be embraced in this last direction, and they will be regulated accordingly; the top and sole of the loop-hole receiving a suitable slope or direction for this purpose.

The foregoing details can only be well determined upon from the special object to which the loop-holed defences are to be applied. Care only is to be taken that in attempting to give cover to the troops their field of view be not too restricted by too narrow an opening for the use of the fire-arms.

Where the throat or narrowest part of the loop-hole is within the wall, the exterior opening leaves a wider mark for the missiles of the assailed, and when the sides of the loop-hole gradually widen outwards, a shot striking one of them may glance inward and do injury.

To prevent this accident, the sides and sometimes the sole are made in offsets. A more convenient form for construction, and one better adapted to arresting the enemy's balls, is to make the exterior portion rectangular in plan for half the width of the wall as already described.

**17. Exterior Corridors.** In open exterior corridors the troops are covered in front either by an earthen parapet, which is usually only musket-proof, the scarp wall being run up to the superior slope; or else the scarp wall serves as the cover, in which case it is pierced either throughout its length or at suitable points with loop-holes. The floor of the corridor, C, Pl. 4, Fig. 27, serves as a banquette tread for the loop-holes, and is therefore placed with reference to the direction of the fire from the loop-holes. The height at which the scarp wall rises above the floor of the corridor will depend upon the level of the floor, and that of the bottom of the ditch; this height, however, should not be less than 6½ feet to afford a sufficient cover to the troops.

The preceding Fig. is given as an example of a semi-detached scarp, A, an earthen counterscarp and covered way, D; being a section of an outwork of one of our sea-coast forts.

**18. Barbette Batteries.** For guns mounted on the ordinary field and siege carriages, the barbettes are constructed in the same manner and with the same dimensions as in field works; the arrangement of the ramps and slopes being determined by the position in which the barbette is placed, and its relative position with respect to the terre-plein and parapet.

For the heavy guns used in forts, both for sea and land fronts, a solid foundation of stone is laid to receive the pintle and rail upon which the chassis of the gun is made to traverse. This foundation consists of a heavy block set firmly in a bed of beton to which the pintle, placed at the centre of motion, is solidly attached; and of stone blocks set in like manner, to which are firmly attached the iron rails, which either form a segment of a circle as in Pl. 7, Figs. 54, 55, or a complete circle, as in Figs. 56, 57, 58, upon which the traverse wheels run.

In order to afford the gun a wide traverse, a recess is made in the parapet in front of the carriage, of sufficient dimensions to allow the manœuvres of the chassis and top carriage without obstruction; for this purpose it has received a depth of 2 feet, its front 5 feet; its two sides having a slant of 30 inches base to 24 inches perpendicular. The recess and usually the entire length of the battery front is faced with a breast-high wall that only rises within 18 inches of the top of the parapet; its thickness being 2 feet. The Figs. referred to give the plan, sections, and elevation of the barbette arrangements in question, adopted in our service.

**19. Embrasure Batteries.** The embrasures cut in the parapets for guns on field and siege carriages differ in no essential point from those for field works. It is well, however, to observe, as the parapet is weakened by receiving embrasures, the splay given to them should, in all cases, be carefully regulated by the field of fire it is desirable to command, so as to leave as large a mass of merlon between each as practicable, to resist the assailant's fire.

For guns mounted on sea-coast carriages the embrasures are very shallow, merely covering the gun from lateral view.

**20. Machicoulis.** For the purpose of attaining, by musketry, the foot of a scarp wall without flank defences, resort must be had to a machicoulated arrangement at the top of the scarp.

The usual mode adopted for this purpose, Pl. 8, Figs. 67, 68, is to form a parapet wall which rests upon a solid horizontal band of stone, near the top of the scarp, which is supported on corbels or projecting blocks, firmly built into the wall. The back of the parapet wall is placed a few inches in advance of the scarp, leaving room for the slanting loop-holes pierced in the horizontal band through which the fire is to be delivered on the foot of the scarp. The top of the parapet wall is also arranged to admit of firing on more distant points.

In the example given, which is from an Austrian authority, Fig. 67 is a front elevation, and Fig. 68 a section through a loop-hole.

Figs. 65, 66 are a front elevation and section through a loop-hole, from the same authority. This is a semi-detached scarp wall, the top portion of which is arranged on the back with loop-hole recesses; the lower portion having very inclined arched recesses in front, with slanting loop-holes to fire on the foot of the scarp from the upper recesses.

Where from the irregularity of the site, the ordinary machicoulis cannot be made efficient, resort may be had to small polygonal chambers of stone, open at top, and having the sides and bottom pierced with loop-holes and machicoulis. These constructions may be made just of sufficient size to hold a single sentinel. They are placed at the angles of the works where they will not be exposed to artillery, and are supported on a corbel work projecting from the top of the scarp wall.

## IV.

### COVERED DEFENCES.

**21. Detached Scarp Walls,** When the scarp walls are entirely detached, leaving an open corridor between them and the rampart, they are pierced with one or two tiers of loop-holes, from which a fire can be brought upon the ditch and upon the terre-plein of the covered-way, or any work in front of the enceinte.

To give cover to the men at the loop-holes arched recesses, Pl. 4, Figs. 25, 26, are made in the thickness of wall, or else short counterforts are built back from the wall, which serve as the piers of covering arches. The width of the recesses should admit of three or four loop-holes at the usual distance apart, their height and depth being sufficient to give the men shelter from vertical fire and allow them to handle their arms with convenience.

The two Figs. above are sections of this description of scarp wall taken through the crowns of the arches, as shown in an Austrian work. A is a section of the wall; B and D, elevations of the sides of the recesses; C, an elevation and section of the recess arch.

**22. Semi-detached Walls,** Fig. 28, are also in some cases built with recesses. Besides these, traverse walls, H, are built back from the scarp wall into the parapet, at intervals, to afford cover to troops, circulating in the corridor, from enfilading fire, and to admit of a defence of the corridor if the assailant should enter it between any two of these traverses. For this purpose they are pierced with loop-holes, and have door-ways for circulation throughout the corridor.

**23. Scarp Galleries.** In the permanent works of more recent construction in our own country and in Europe revetment walls with relieving arches, Pl. 4, Fig. 15, have in most cases been introduced instead of the ordinary thick walls with counterforts, which had been hitherto the usual mode of retaining the earth of the rampart and parapet.

The piers of the relieving arches, which also serve as counterforts to the revetment-wall, are rectangular in plan, and usually run back from 12 to 16 feet. They are from 4 to 6 feet thick, and placed from 12 to 18 feet apart between their centre lines. The arches are usually full centre and 2 feet thick, with a rough shaped capping which adds an additional thickness from 9 to 12 inches over the crown of the arch.

The preceding Fig. is a section of a revetment wall of this kind, of one of our forts, through the curtain in front of which is a mask of which D is the section. B is an elevation of the face of the pier; C, the relieving arch; and A, the scarp wall.

This mode of construction offers the advantages of a more stable structure and rendering it more difficult for the assailant to make a practicable breach in the wall, whilst by a suitable arrangement of the relieving arches and their piers with the earth of the rampart, a sufficient space can be secured behind the scarp wall to form a gallery for defensive purposes.

The arches and piers form the top and sides of the gallery, the scarp wall forming the front, and the back or rear being either partly or wholly closed by a wall which retains the earth behind it. The gallery is thus divided up into chambers, the communication between which is effected by doorways made through the piers.

The width and height of the gallery should in all cases be sufficient to allow the men ample room for handling their fire-arms, and to admit of a circulation through the gallery when the troops for the defence are posted in it.

From three to four loop-holes are made in the portion of the scarp wall that forms the front of each chamber. The dimensions and forms of the loop-holes are the same as already described, and they are otherwise arranged for defence as in detached scarp walls.

In Pl. 4, Fig. 16, a section of a scarp gallery constructed in one of our forts is shown. A is the scarp wall; B the pier of the relieving arch C; D the rear wall which closes the gallery and sustains the earth behind it. The section also shows the parts of the rampart and parapet and the breast-high wall E.

In Figs. 17, 18, 19, the plan, section, and rear elevation of a gallery are shown as given in French authorities. The peculiarity of this example, Fig. 19, consists in the arrangement of the rear of the gallery, which, instead of being entirely closed by a wall, is only partly so; a small wall, a, which rests upon an arch, b, built between the two piers, is placed parallel to the back of the scarp wall and at a distance from it equal to the width of the gallery, the top of the wall being raised to the level of the surface of the earthen slope which falls in behind from the top of the arch.

The section, Fig. 18, through r s, and elevation, Fig. 19, show the position of the loop-holes, and the vent for the escape of the smoke is pierced in the scarp wall just below the crown of the arch. B are the piers; A the arches with their capping; D the doorways through the piers.

Figs. 20, 21, represent the plan and section of a scarp gallery in two tiers, as given in an Austrian work. The rear of the gallery is closed by a simple wall. Besides the vent holes for the escape of smoke, drains are made in the scarp wall at the level of the gallery floor to convey off any water that may collect in it.

Figs. 22, 23, are a plan and section, from the same authority, of a gallery behind the lower portion of the scarp wall, the upper portion being connected with relieving arches so arranged that, being open to the rear, the foot of the slope of earth will just touch the back of the wall at its foot within. In this example the pressure of the earth being supposed to be great, the gallery is closed in the rear by arched walls; the arches being built into the vertical piers B, of the relieving arches C. This example also shows the manner of barricading the doorways through the piers by vertical grooves, made in the opposite faces of the piers, to receive the scantling forming the barricade.

In Fig. 28 is shown the section of a gallery behind the lower portion of the scarp, with the upper portion arranged with recesses for loop-holes.

**24. Counterscarp Galleries.** Pl. 4, Fig. 35. The most simple method of arranging a gallery behind a counterscarp wall for the defence of a ditch, is to build another wall parallel to that of the counterscarp, and to throw an arch over between the two to cover the top of the gallery. The counterscarp wall is pierced with loop-holes arranged in the same way as in scarp galleries.

The example selected is from one of our works, and shows a section of the gallery through a loop-hole. A, counterscarp wall; D, parallel wall; C, arch and capping; E, glacis mask covering the scarp wall.

In Figs. 29, 30, 31, are shown a plan, section on r s, and a section and interior elevation on o p, of a counterscarp gallery taken from a French authority. In this case counterforts, square in plan, are built along the back of the counterscarp wall, leaving 8 feet between them. Parallel to the counterscarp wall and 4 feet in rear of the counterforts another wall is built, which, with the counterforts, serves as the support of a series of arches perpendicular to the counterscarp wall sprung between the counterforts, and another parallel to it and resting on the counterfort and parallel wall. The arches between the counterforts form with them recesses, A, for the men serving the loop-holes pierced in the counterscarp wall; whilst the covered space, B, in rear serves for circulation without disturbing the men engaged in firing.

Counterscarp galleries may also be arranged for a ditch defence with artillery, short guns like carronades being used for this purpose. A plan, Fig. 32, a vertical section and side elevation on D C, Fig. 33; and a section and back elevation on A B, Fig. 34, taken from one of our works, show a disposition of this kind in the reëntering angle of the counterscarp.

**25. Bastionnets.** In small works, where a flanking disposition cannot be obtained from the enceinte, as in lunettes and redoubts, the ditches may be swept by covered chambers, Pl. 5, Fig. 39, attached to the scarp wall either at the centre of the sides of the work, or at the angles.

These chambers, Pl. 5, Fig. 39, are usually of a pentagonal form, the sides which join the scarp wall serving to flank it, and the two exterior sides, forming a salient angle, delivering their fire on the opposite counterscarp and its crest. From their form and purposes they have received the name of bastionnets.

The dimensions of these constructions will depend upon the amount and kind of fire to be delivered. Their scarps should be as high as that of the main work. The entrance to them is either directly from a parade by a postern, or from a scarp gallery which flanks them.

Fig. 39 shows a plan of bastionnet, D, at an angle, communicating with a scarp gallery, E. In rear of the scarp gallery and opposite to the bastionnet, is placed a small powder magazine for its service. The example is from Austrian authority, and is arranged for one small gun on each flank, besides the loop-holes for small-arms.

As a general rule it may be laid down that the salient angles of the redoubt are the most suitable positions for the bastionnets, as they will thus form small bastioned fronts, in which both the sides of the main work and those of the bastionnet will be swept by the flanks of the latter. The only danger in this arrangement is that the loop-holes in one flank may be fired into from the opposite one. This, however, may be guarded against by a suitable position given to the loop-holes.

As the main object of covered defences is protection against shells, it is essential that the arches of the galleries and bastionnets should be bomb-proof. As the span of these arches is usually small, a thickness of 2 feet given to the masonry and a covering from 4 to 6 feet of earth above it, are ordinarily considered sufficient for the object in view.

With regard to the front walls of these constructions, as they are too thin to withstand the direct action of artillery, they must either be covered by earthen masks, as a glacis raised beyond the counterscarp for example, or be used only in positions where they are not exposed to this fire.

**General Remarks.** It should be observed that whatever advantages covered defences afford as shelter from the assailant's fire, they present the inconveniences of a comparatively narrow and obstructed field of view to the assailed, which is further obscured by the smoke which may gather within the gallery, and in front of the loopholes. From these causes the assailed having to aim at a venture, his fire is likely to be less effective than in open defences, where the smoke disperses rapidly and leaves a clear field of view. The same may be said of loopholed walls covering exterior corridors where the space to the rear is confined.

Owing to these considerations, loop-holed and covered defences of the kind in question should be restricted to special defensive purposes, where an object within the field of fire can be attained with some certainty whether seen or not by the assailed; as, for example, the protection of a ditch, or a scarp wall which cannot be flanked from within the work ; for sweeping a covered-way, or the interior of any outwork which cannot be brought well under the fire of the parapet of the main work.

**26. Caponnière Defences for the Enceinte Ditch.** These works are classed under the head of what are termed *defensive casemates*, which are bomb-proof arched structures for receiving cannon, firing through embrasures pierced in the front or mask wall of the casemates. Defences of this class, when used to flank the ditch, are usually termed *casemated caponnières.*

**27.** These defences are usually placed in the ditch at the middle point of the side or front to be flanked. The outline of their plan is mostly that of a lunette, Pl. 5, Fig. 36, the flanks being perpendicular to the line of the scarp, and the two faces making a salient angle of 60°. The caponnière is either built in juxtaposition with the enceinte, or else detached from it. In the latter case an inclosure is formed between the two by a loop-holed wall which connects the flanks with the scarp wall. Each flank consists of one or two tiers of arched chambers, the piers of the arches being perpendicular to the back of the walls of the flank. Each chamber is of sufficient dimensions for the service of a single gun with a contracted field of fire. (Pl. 5, Figs. 36, 37.) In some cases loop-holes are pierced for small-arms on each side of the embrasure; in others the casemates of one story are pierced for cannon, and the other for small-arms.

The casemates are closed in rear by a thin wall, which is provided with windows for light and ventilation; and the piers are pierced with doorways to form a communication between the chambers and to assist the ventilation. Flues or vents, Fig. 37, are made in the front wall, just under the arches, for a like purpose. Where it may be necessary the lower floor is drained by a conduit through the front wall.

An open court is left between the flanks, and each flank is covered at top with from 4 to 6 feet of earth. The flanks are separated from the faces by a closed corridor which serves as a communication.

In front of the corridor and on each side of the axis of the caponnière, a casemated chamber, which is open in front, is arranged for one mortar, Figs. 36, 38. The arches of these chambers rise towards the front the better to subserve the object in view.

On one side of the chambers the powder magazine is placed, with a store-room. On the other side a stairway between the stories is built.

The space within the salient angle, inclosed by the walls of the faces and the front of the mortar casemates, is open at top. It has an open corridor on the second story for communication, and the front walls are arranged with loop-holed recesses for small-arms, Figs. 36, 38.

The enceinte, in the rear of the flanks of the caponnière, is arranged with a scarp gallery, to flank the caponnière flanks and the court between them. A break is in some cases made in the line of the scarp wall, perpendicular to the caponnière faces, and casemates for cannon and small-arms arranged behind the scarp wall, to flank these faces. In some cases these flanking dispositions are placed in front of the scarp wall, the casemates being open to the rear, looking on a narrow court between them and the scarp which is closed on the sides by a loop-holed wall.

The example here given of a casemated caponnière is from an Austrian authority. Fig. 36, is the plan; Fig. 37, a section and elevation on A B of one flank, and the end wall of the corridor looking towards the court between the flanks; Fig. 38, a section and elevation along C′ D′ of the corridor, mortar casemate and triangular court. Figs. 37, 38, are on an enlarged scale.

**28. Casemates on Land Fronts.** Various modes have, from time to time, been proposed for arranging defensive casemates for the exterior defence of land fronts. The difficulty in covering the masonry from the batteries of the assailant has been the chief objection to these structures, and is the more prominent as the fire of artillery becomes more accurate, as such casemates would soon be ruined or rendered untenable by embrasure shots.

The structure for this purpose which has been most applied within late years is what is termed the *Haxo casematè;* the details having been first proposed by General Haxo, one of the first authorities of the French school of engineers. These casemates consist, Figs. 45, 46, 47, of a series of arched bomb-proof chambers closed in front by a thin mask wall which, except around the embrasures through it, is covered from the assailant's artillery by the parapet. To present but a small surface of masonry to fire, the arches, which are horizontal and perpendicular to the mask wall for the greater portion of their length, descend towards the front, leaving where they join the mask wall just sufficient height within for the service of the gun. To effect this the anterior portion of the arch must be conoidal in shape.

The piers of the arches are pierced with wide arched openings which serve the double purpose of a communication between the casemates and to give the gun a wider traverse for firing.

Embrasures are pierced in the parapet in prolongation of those of the mask wall, and it is proposed to cover the small portion of the masonry necessarily exposed by this arrangement by placing several thicknesses of heavy timber in front of it to receive the shot, or to case it with wrought-iron.

When the casemates serve simply for the cover of the cannon, the arches are covered with from 4 to 6 feet thickness of earth, and are left open to the rear for the more prompt escape of the smoke, and a ditch is sometimes made just in rear of the casemates to catch bombs and limit the effects of their explosion. When the arches are made longer than for the service of the guns alone, the earthen covering is sometimes arranged with a parapet to cover cannon in barbette, or for small-arms.

The example shown by the Figs. is from a French authority. Fig. 45 is a plan on m n, Fig. 47; Fig. 46 a section and interior elevation towards the mask wall on o p, Fig. 47; and Fig. 47 a section and side elevation on r s, Fig. 45, 46.

In Figs. 48, 49, is shown an arrangement of two casemates of the Haxo kind from an Austrian authority. In this case the masonry is covered on the flanks from enfilading fire by earth. Fig. 48 is an interior elevation of the arches, and the back wall that retains the earth on the sides. Fig. 49 is a longitudinal section, and shows the manner of covering the masonry in front and securing the earthen embrasure by a timber facing.

**29. Mortar Casemates.** In Fig. 50, Pl. 6, is shown a longitudinal section of a mortar casemate placed in rear of a parapet, by which it is covered from direct fire. The arch is covered, as in the preceding case, by earth, to break the shock of shells. It rises towards the front to give ample room for the shell in its flight. The casemates are covered on their flanks from enfilading fire by an embankment, and are partly closed by a wall in the rear. A small ditch is made in front of the chamber, and a slight wall built within it, to give cover from the splinters of shells falling between the parapet and the casemate. Arched chambers are in some cases made beneath the mortar chambers which serve as store rooms and temporary magazines.

When these casemates are placed in rear of a portion of the parapet but little exposed to direct fire, the thickness of the parapet in front of them may be reduced, and the interior slope be replaced by a breast-high wall along the front of the casemates, in order to give better cover in flank and from slant fire, by throwing forward the casemates more under cover of the parapet.

The example given is from the same authority as in the preceding example of casemated caponnières.

**30. Casemates for Water Fronts.** In the casemated batteries for sea-coast and harbor defences, the scarp or mask walls of the chambers for the guns, being exposed to the fire of ships alone, are not covered, as on land fronts, by an earthen mask; these walls being built of sufficient thickness and strength to withstand the fire of the heaviest guns within the range that ships can venture to attack, and being far less vulnerable than the wooden or iron sides of vessels thus far brought into general use.

These batteries in our own and European works consist of a series of arched bomb-proof chambers which serve for the service of the guns alone; or else they receive such dimensions that the portions of the chambers immediately in rear of the mask wall are appropriated to the service of the battery, and the rear portions are converted into quarters, store rooms, and other necessary purposes for the garrison.

In the earlier sea-coast casemated defences constructed in our service, the gun chambers have received dimensions to admit of two guns in each chamber, Pl. 5, Figs. 40, 41. The chambers are usually formed of segmental brick arches of 120°, which rest upon stone piers built back perpendicular to the mask wall. In the example given, the arches, C, have a uniform thickness of 3 feet exclusive of the roof-shaped capping, which is generally of rubble and beton, and covered on top by the earth of the parapet and rampart. The stone piers, E, are 6½ feet thick, and are pierced with arched communications, F, a few feet in rear of the mask wall, so placed as to give the gun carriage a wider traverse by allowing it to run under this opening. Arched recesses, E, are made in the mask wall to admit the muzzle of the gun being well run out, so as to clear the casemate of smoke. An embrasure, e, is pierced at the centre of each recess, the sole being at the proper height above the floor of the casemate, to accommodate the casemate chassis and top carriage. In Fig. 40 are shown the plan and dimensions of the embrasure usually adopted in our works until a very recent date; and in Fig. 41, which is a vertical section of the casemate through the axis of an embrasure, are shown the elevation and dimensions of the cheeks, e, of the embrasure. In the casemates of some of our works, flues for ventilation and carrying off rapidly the powder smoke run from the top of the carriage recesses, E, through the masonry of the scarp wall, and have their outlet in the top of the wall. In others the flues run from the casemate arch to the top of the parapet. Beneath the embrasure a recess, termed the *tongue hole*, which in plan is triangular, is made to receive the tongue of the chassis. The tongue is confined in its place, and the chassis traverses around a pintle which is received into the *pintle hole* made at the centre point of the throat of the embrasure, and extending into the masonry below the tongue hole.

When the casemates serve also as quarters for the garrison, the rear, towards the parade, is closed by a brick or stone parade wall, which forms the front wall of the quarters. A brick partition wall separates the quarters from the gun gallery. Arched recesses and flues are made in the piers for chimneys, and the parade wall, the sides of the piers, and soffit of the arch, are suitably finished to give a dry and well ventilated dwelling.

In the example here given, as in most of our earlier casemated works, there is but one tier of casemated guns; this tier being surmounted by a barbette battery covered either by an earthen or stone parapet on the water fronts.

Casemates adapted to two guns in each room present a more vulnerable mark in the portion of the mask wall between the piers; expose more men to danger from embrasure shots; present a greater opening in rear to the assailant's fire when not closed by a parade wall; offer less resistance to the shock of shells; and are more difficult to construct without settling than rooms for single guns. These advantages in favor of casemates for single guns are the more marked where, for the purpose of obtaining a heavy fire in some fixed direction, it is desirable to resort to a castellated structure consisting of several tiers of casemates.

In Pl. 6, Figs. 42, 43, 44, is shown a plan, Fig. 42, on E F of the first tier of casemates; a vertical section and side elevation, Fig. 43, on A B, of the three tiers of casemates and the top barbette battery; and in Fig. 44 an interior elevation on C D; of one of the most recent of these structures for the defence of the channel leading to one of our harbors. Besides the wide arched openings, F, through the piers, for communication and the traverse of the guns, smaller doorways, a, are made for communications in rear of the battery. The casemates are open in the rear. The arches of the top tier are alone made bomb-proof; those of the lower tiers being of sufficient strength to receive the armament and admit of the service of the guns with safety.

**31. Embrasures.** The form, dimensions, and construction of embrasures in mask walls present a problem which has offered no little difficulty, in a satisfactory solution, to engineers, by which the best cover could be given to the guns and men by exposing the least surface to embrasure shots, whilst the guns should receive a suitable traverse to command a wide field of fire.

In the embrasures of our works the general form is the same as those usually found in Europe, but they present a very considerably less amount of exterior and throat opening than European embrasures. See Pl. 7, Fig. 59, which is the plan of a French carriage recess and embrasure for a single gun, and Fig. 60, which is one of the same parts of an English fort for sea-coast defence. In some of our earlier works the sole, cheeks, and top of the embrasures are constructed of brick, as being a material that would be less destructive through the splinters driven in by embrasure shots. This view, however, has been abandoned in our more recent works, the embrasures being constructed, on the contrary, of heavy stone blocks carefully and strongly bonded; a brick arch being thrown above the embrasure within the mass of the mask wall to secure the upper portion from yielding, should the block forming the ceiling of the embrasure be damaged.

A further and most important step has been more recently taken, in the application to embrasures of wrought-iron casings and throat pieces, with shutters of the same material, as a security against heavy shot and grape. The first application of this means has been made to the embrasures of one of our works now in the course of construction; and the forms, dimensions, and construction of the embrasures are the results of experiments carefully made with the heaviest solid shot and grape, upon walls and embrasures of various forms and dimensions, under the directions of General Totten, Chief Engineer.

The form adopted is shown in plan in Pl. 8, Fig. 61, the interior portion being trapezoidal, and the exterior beyond the throat rectangular. This form was adopted with the double view of limiting the effects of embrasure shot which, in the old forms, striking the oblique surface of the cheeks of the exterior portion and glancing inwards, occasioned considerable casualties; and to form a suitable recess for strong iron shutters to protect from grape entering through the throat whilst the gun was out of battery. The two principal wrought-iron throat pieces are trapezoidal in plan, being 8 inches thick and 17 inches base, the oblique side having the same slant as the inner cheek of the embrasure. Exterior to these two pieces are two plate pieces, each two inches thick, against which the shutters, which are also two inches thick, rest when open or closed, as shown in Fig. 61. There is also a wrought-iron plate casing around the exterior opening of the embrasure, as shown in Fig. 61, and in the exterior elevation, Fig. 64. In Fig. 62 is shown an interior elevation of the carriage recess, the embrasure and the tongue-hole; and in Fig. 63 a vertical section and side elevation on A B, Fig. 64, of the embrasure, carriage recess, and the pintle and tongue holes.

The exterior width of the embrasure, the obliquity given to the cheeks of the interior portion, and the depth and slant given to the carriage recess and its sides, are arranged with a view to the traverse of the gun, which is fixed at 60°, or 30° on each side of the axis of the embrasure.

All the parts of the wall adjacent to the embrasure are constructed of the largest sized block of the toughest stone, the blocks being carefully fitted and bonded, and having the additional strength afforded by a very ingenious arrangement of hollow bolts and a concrete of lead and chippings of stone run together. A brick arch, as shown in the elevations and sections, is turned over the embrasure and within the mass of the scarp wall.

**32. Bomb-proof Buildings.** Casemated bomb-proof quarters are indispensable to the safety and comfort of the garrison during siege, or any prolonged attack for the annoyance or reduction of the work by a bombardment. In small works like most of our forts, which are chiefly designed for sea-coast defence, casemated quarters are arranged, as has been seen, in the rear of the batteries, a portion of each casemate towards the parade being partitioned off and suitably disposed for the object in view. In some cases, advantage is taken of a scarp wall, on a land front, which is well covered by a glacis or other face cover, to form in its rear quarters of this character. In all cases, care should be taken to place such quarters on those fronts which are best covered from a direct fire, and the parade walls of which are not exposed to reverse fire. Whenever the plan of the work admits of it, quarters of this kind should be arranged for defence, by being pierced with loopholes and even with embrasures for cannon. Defensive casemated quarters form a prominent and distinctive feature in what is now known as the German school of permanent fortification. They consist of bomb-proof buildings of a curvilinear or polygonal plan, arranged for one or more stories of covered defences, with an ordinary open defence surmounting the casemates. The casemates of the upper stories are covered with bomb-proof arches, whilst those of the lower stories receive flat segment arches of only sufficient thickness and strength to bear the weight of the guns, and to subserve the other objects of the structure. When employed as caponnières, as gorge defences, or as interior retrenchments, the front walls of these structures are masked from direct views, either by the glacis, or by the parapet of the work in which they are placed, and they receive a thickness of at least 5 feet. But as a mask wall even of this thickness, when pierced with loop-holes and embrasures, is liable to damage from shot which plunge over the parapet in front of it, Pl. 7, Fig. 53, the portions of the casemate piers, B, where they join the mask wall, A, are made thicker, in some cases, for a distance of a few feet back, than their general thickness, in order to receive two vertical grooves in the face of this thicker portion, into which scantling being inserted horizontally, and the space between the two partitions thus formed filled in with sand bags or other shot-proof materials, a temporary shelter can be formed when the ruin of the mask wall exposes the interior of the casemate to view. In our service, Pl. 7, Figs. 51, 52, when casemated quarters are constructed of two stories, the upper one alone is covered with a bomb-proof arch, the floor between the two being of timber and constructed in the ordinary way.

In Fig. 51 is shown a plan on A D, Fig. 52, of bomb-proof casemated quarters in rear of a scarp wall, and of a counterscarp gallery, both arranged with loop-holed defences. Fig. 52 is a section and side elevation on C D, Fig. 51, showing the rampart and parapet over the arch, and the fire-places and chimneys in the piers of the arches. The floor of the second story is of timber. The rear or parade wall is pierced with doors and windows.

In Fig. 53 is shown the plan of the end of a casemated defensive barrack from an Austrian authority. The front wall, A, is arranged and pierced for cannon, each arched chamber for one gun. The end wall is loop-holed for musketry, and the rear wall, C, has windows and doors.

**33. Powder Magazine.** The structures for this purpose are built with strong, full centre bomb-proof brick arches, supported on heavy stone piers which form the outward walls, and to which interior buttresses are sometimes added. The capping of the arches is covered with from 4 to 6 feet of solidly packed earth. The interior of the magazine, the floors, and the doors and windows, are built with a view to security from fire; and to preserve the powder from dampness, by a good system of drainage around the foundations, and of ventilation by means of air-holes made through the piers, and panels of copper pierced with small holes placed in the doors. No iron or steel fastening or sheeting is allowed in any part of the structure; and in arranging the air-holes through the piers they receive a broken direction, and have a copper mesh-work placed across them, to prevent any combustible material, or rats or mice, penetrating to the interior of the magazine.

In large works the magazines are isolated as far as practicable from the enceinte, so as not to endanger it should an accidental explosion take place. The magazine is inclosed by a strong high wall for security, and is provided with lightning rods. In small works some one or more of the casemates in the position least exposed to the assailant's fire are built for the purposes of a magazine.

## V.

### COMMUNICATIONS.

**34. General Remarks.** The communications form a very important element in the defence of permanent works. The size and disposition] of the communications should vary with the character of the work in which they are placed.

In small works, which from the size of their garrisons are calculated to make only a strictly passive defence, communications of just sufficient dimensions for the passage of the troops from point to point will serve every purpose, and can be more easily barricaded and otherwise defended.

But for large works having full garrisons, the communications should be such that sorties of all arms and in large bodies can be quickly made. With communications of this character a besieging force would be constrained to adopt extraordinary measures of safety, keeping large guards in the trenches to secure them from such sorties, to which they would be continually exposed.

**35.** All communications, to serve properly their ends, should fulfil the following conditions:

1. *They should never, from their position, compromise the safety of the enceinte.*

Frequent instances could be cited of works which have been surprised by an enemy obtaining possession of the gates. Therefore too many precautions cannot be taken to secure the principal outlet from the body of the place, from similar attempts. It is on this account, that the postern and gateway in the main entrance are arranged as has been described, to frustrate any sudden attack that might be made upon it.

2. *They should admit of a convenient circulation of the besieged.*

To subserve this purpose, the dimensions, slopes, etc., of the posterns, ramps, and other similar works, should be convenient for the service to which they are applied; and they should be placed in such positions as lead directly to the point to be arrived at.

3. *The position chosen for any communication should be such that when an enemy gets possession of it, he may obtain no advantage by it.*

To be useless to an enemy, the communication, when in his possession, should not offer a shelter for his works; nor enable him to carry them on with more ease. This end will be obtained by placing the communications in a position to be enfiladed by the fire of the works in their rear; and so arranging them as to preserve the counterscarp wall unbroken.

4. *The communications should be covered from every point where an enemy might establish himself, during the whole period that they can be of service to the besieged; and they should be swept by the fire of the enceinte.*

Without these precautions, an enemy might cut off all communication from the enceinte with the outworks; and in case of retreat, the troops could not derive any assistance from the enceinte, if he attempted to press upon them.

5. *They should be so placed as not to compromise the retreat of the troops.*

This is effected by placing the communication in the re-enterings, which are the most secure points; as an enemy to arrive at them will have to brave a powerful column of flank fire. Barriers, gates, and movable bridges of timber should be placed at suitable points, to cut off one communication from another; and thus arrest the progress of a pursuing enemy.

6. *Finally, each work should be independent of every communication, except that one destined for its particular use.*

This is an important object, as it prevents an enemy, should he succeed in gaining possession of a communication leading through it, from seizing upon the work itself.

**36. Ramps.** The principal communications consist of *ramps*, *stairs*, *posterns*, *gateways*, *bridges*, and, for wet ditches, *dikes.* The width of ramps at top for the service of the artillery and other vehicles may be from 10 to 15 feet, and their inclination from $\frac{1}{6}$ to $_{15}$, or less, depending on the difference of level to be overcome. They are usually placed in positions where they will occupy the least room of the parade, as along the rampart slope of the enceinte. As a general rule, their side slopes are of earth; but where it is desirable to economize room on the parade the side slopes are replaced on one or both sides by a wall which sustains the earth of the ramp. When ramps serve for infantry alone their width may be reduced to 6 feet, and in some cases to 4 feet.

**37. Stairs.** Except for temporary purposes, stairs are constructed of stone; each step being a solid block which is 6 feet long in the clear; its breadth at top or the tread 12 inches, and its height or rise 8 inches. Stairs are usually placed along the counterscarp and gorge walls of the outworks, forming a communication, for infantry only, between the ditch and the terre plein of the work to which they lead. They are also used within the enceinte in positions where there is not sufficient room for ramps; or where, for greater security from surprise, it is desirable to present a narrower and more difficult defile to the assailant. In cases where room is wanting and the communication not in habitual use, the width of the stair may be reduced to 4 feet.

**38. Posterns.** Posterns are arched bomb-proof passage-ways constructed under the terre-pleins and ramparts, forming subterranean communications between the parade and the enceinte ditch, or between the ditches and the interior of the outworks. The width and height of the interior of posterns depend upon the use to which the communication is to be applied. For artillery the width is usually taken at 10 feet, and the height under the crown or key of the arch at least 8 feet. Posterns for infantry may be only from 6 to 4 feet wide, and from 6 feet 6 inches to 8 feet high under the crown of the arch. The thickness of the piers of the arches is generally taken at about half the width of the postern. The arches are from 18 inches to two feet thick. As any injury to the arch from the bursting of a shell over it might obstruct the communication, the arch should be covered with a thickness of at least 3 feet of earth, and when convenient with 5 or 6 feet for greater security. A strong wooden door is placed at each outlet of the postern

3

to secure it against surprise. The doorway in posterns for the service of artillery should be of just sufficient height for the convenient passage of a gun; about 7 feet for each dimension is usually allowed for this purpose.

The most important postern is the one leading from the parade to the enceinte ditch. This generally receives a width of 12 feet and the same height under the crown. For greater security from surprise, its outlet at the enceinte ditch is at least 6 feet above the bottom of the ditch, this difference of level being overcome by means of a temporary wooden ramp which receives an inclination of at least $\frac{1}{6}$. With a like object, besides two strong doors at the two ends of the postern, there is a partition of masonry about midway between the two ends, which is pierced with a doorway of the same size as the doorways of the ends, and closed by a strong door which, as well as the partition wall, is loop-holed for musketry.

In cases where the postern forms the main entrance to the work, an arched chamber is placed on one side of it, at the outlet, which serves as a guard-room for a few men, to secure the outlet from surprise. The wall between this chamber and the postern is loop-holed, so that a fire can be brought to bear on the doorway of the postern; and as a further precaution against surprise a machicoulis defence is sometimes arranged at the top of the scarp wall just above the doorway of the postern.

**39. Gateway.** In works with large garrisons, where the means of frequent communication with the exterior are requisite, posterns of ordinary dimensions are found not to afford a sufficient convenience for the daily wants. In such cases a passage-way of sufficient width to admit of at least a single carriage-road with narrow foot-paths on each side has to be opened through the rampart, which, whenever it is practicable to do so, should be arched and covered with earth to render it bomb-proof. The passage-way should for security have the bottom of its outlet at least 12 feet above the bottom of the enceinte ditch; and when this difference of level cannot be obtained the main ditch should be deepened sufficiently for the purpose below the outlet. A gateway of sufficient height and width for the passage of the ordinary vehicles for the service of the garrison is made through the scarp wall. This gateway is arched at top, where a machicoulis defence may also be arranged to guard the outlet on the exterior.

The communication across the enceinte ditch leading

from the gateway is usually an ordinary wooden bridge built on piles. The bay of this bridge at the gateway is spanned by a drawbridge of timber, which when drawn up closes and secures the gateway. This drawbridge is manœuvred by some of the usual mechanisms employed for this purpose.

**40. Port-Cullis.** When the gateway is not preceded by a ditch and is therefore without a drawbridge, a barrier, termed a *port-cullis*, which can be lowered or raised vertically by machinery, is sometimes added to secure the passage-way from surprise. The ancient port-cullis was a framework of heavy beams, placed vertically, leaving a few inches only between each pair of beams. These vertical beams were either solidly confined between horizontal beams, or clamping-pieces in pairs; or else they were so arranged that they could slide upwards between the clamping-pieces. Each of the vertical beams was shod at the bottom with a strong pointed iron shoe. The horizontal pieces were framed securely with two heavy vertical beams that formed the sides of the frame, and were fitted into vertical grooves made in the side walls of the passage-way in which the frame could slide when raised or lowered. By arranging the vertical beams to slide upwards between the clamping pieces, it enabled the passage-way to be closed in cases where an obstruction might be designedly placed below the port-cullis to prevent this being done; as the beams which meet the obstruction would be pushed upwards, whilst the others would fall to their ordinary level and close the passage-way on each side of the obstruction.

In the works recently constructed with us the port-cullis, and even the doors preceding them, have been constructed of a strong open lattice-work of wrought iron bars bolted strongly to the wrought-iron uprights and cross-pieces, forming the framework of the lattice. This is a great improvement for these purposes, both as to durability and defence.

Passage-ways of this description should be secured by all the means at an engineer's disposal. A large guard-room, with loop-holes bearing on the passage, should be erected on one side, near the gateway; and if the enceinte is a simple one, without outworks beyond its ditch, a small lunette, or loop-holed tambour of masonry, or timber, should be constructed beyond the counterscarp, forming a tête-de-pont, for the security of the bridge from surprise.

The drawbridge, which for convenience of manœuvring should not be longer than 12 feet, is constructed in the usual mode. Care should be taken that it should fit the recess in the face of the wall so closely that there will not be room enough between it and the jambs of the gateway to insert a crow-bar to force back the bridge.

## VI.

### ENCEINTES.

**41.** The most simple mode of fortifying a position in a permanent manner consists in inclosing it with a rampart surmounted by a parapet, with a ditch the scarp of which when dry is revetted with masonry, and so covered by an earthen mask that it cannot be breached except by batteries placed on the border of the counterscarp.

This line of fortification enclosing the position is termed the *enceinte*, the *body of the place* or the *main inclosure.*

The general outline of the enceinte may be *curvilinear*, or a *polygonal figure* of any character.

**42. System of Fortification.** Although an infinite diversity of figures may thus be presented in the outline or plan of the enceinte, they may all be classed under four heads, to each of which engineers generally have applied the term *system of fortification.*

These four classes are, 1, the *circular* or *curvilinear system:* 2, the *polygonal* or *caponnière system:* 3, the *tenailled system:* 4, the *bastioned system.*

The term *method of fortification* is now usually applied to the manner of fortifying which is generally prevalent in any country; or to the mode adopted by any individual, as the *German method; Vauban's method, &c.*

**Circular System.** The circular system consists of an enceinte, the plan of which is circular or curvilinear.

**Polygonal System.** In the polygonal system the plan is either a polygon with salient angles alone, Pl. 8, Fig. 72, each side of which, AA, is flanked by a casemated caponnière, C, placed in the ditch, D, and midway between the two salients, A; or else each side of the polygon is broken inwards at the centre, so as to form a slight reëntering, Pl. 8, Figs. 73, 74, 75, 76, 77, to procure a casemated flanking arrangement, FF, for the caponnières, C, which occupy these reënterings, and also, in some cases, to flank works in advance of the enceinte.

**Tenailled System.** The tenailled system, Pl. 8, Fig. 78, consists of a tenailled line, the reëntering angles of which are between 90° and 100°, and the salient angles not less than 60°.

**Bastioned System.** In the bastioned system, Fig. 79, the bastions usually consist of two faces and two flanks, the scarps of each of which are plane surfaces.

In many of the older fortifications, and in a few of the more recent works in Europe, the flank is broken; the portion of it at the shoulder angle forming a projecting mass which is termed an *orillon*, whilst the portion between the orillon and the enceinte curtain is retired, or brought in towards the interior of the bastion, and is thus partially covered by the orillon from fire, except in the prolongation of the enceinte ditch. In some cases the plan of the orillon as well as that of the retired flank is curvilinear; in others they are both rectilinear.

**43. General Remarks.** Whatever system may be adopted for the enceinte, there are certain conditions, in addition to those already laid down for all permanent works, which it must satisfy to render it effective:

1. *It should have a steep revetted scarp; unbroken on all sides except for the necessary openings for communications; thoroughly flanked throughout by cannon and small-arms; and of sufficient height to prevent all ordinary attempts at escalade.*

2. *The scarp should be so covered by earthen or other masks that it cannot be reached by the projectiles of an assailant from any position exterior to these masks.*

3. *The parapet and interior covered shelters should be proof against solid and hollow loaded projectiles.*

4. *The parapet should command all the site and outworks exterior to the enceinte and within range of its guns, and sweep them with flank and cross-fires.*

5. *As far as practicable, the principal lines of the parapet should receive such directions, that the assailant cannot take up positions to enfilade them.*

Every enceinte, whatever be the system adopted, will be more or less effective as these conditions are more or less complied with in its arrangement.

## VII.

### OUTWORKS.

**44.** A work consisting of an enceinte alone is more or less exposed to surprise, as it must have outlets of some description to keep up a communication with the exterior, and a bridge, or other means for crossing the ditch.

But this is not the only defect of a fortification of this simple character; for having no covers beyond the ditch for its garrison, their action must be restricted to what may be termed a passive resistance alone; in any attempt to operate on the exterior, they are exposed to fire as soon as they emerge from the ditch, and in a retreat towards the work, if closely pursued by the assailant, they will not only run the risk of being cut off, but a retreat under such circumstances may lead to the capture of the work itself, by the assailant being enabled to enter it with the retreating force.

To provide against dangers of so grave a character, engineers have devised other defences beyond the ditch, and which they have placed in immediate defensive relations with the enceinte, being under its fire, and in positions where, if assaulted, they can be readily succored by the garrison. To this class of exterior defences the term *outworks* has been applied.

From their position, exterior to the enceinte, and from their angular form, so as to be flanked by it, the outworks, with the enceinte, form salient and reëntering parts, which are very favorable to the security of sortie parties in retiring; and as, if properly arranged, the assailant must take them in succession, they will greatly prolong the defence, by forcing him to a great development of his trenches; through which, in some of the positions he will be obliged to occupy, he will be the enveloped party Besides this, he will be obliged to establish breach batteries against each work in succession, always a difficult and perilous task.

**45.** The outworks should satisfy the following conditions to render them effective and secure.

1. *They should have revetted scarps of sufficient height to secure them from any ordinary open assault.*

2. *As far as practicable their scarps should be flanked by the enceinte, and be masked from the positions of the assailant's batteries.*

3. *Their parapets and covered shelters should be shot-proof.*

4. *Those which are most retired should command those in advance; and whenever this cannot be done the retired work should be defiled from the one in advance by which it is commanded.*

5. *In any combination of outworks the dispositions should be such that the more advanced ones shall fall into the hands of the assailant before he will be able to gain possession of the more retired.*

6. *The communications should be ample, and satisfy the general conditions for these elements.*

**46.** The works which come under this head are the *covered-way*, the *tenaille*, the *demi-lune*, the *counterguard*, the *redoubt* or *réduit*, the *tenaillon*, the *horn-work*, and the *crown-work*.

**47. Covered-Way.** The covered-way, as its name imports, is an open corridor or passage, masked from the assailant's view by an embankment, which borders the ditch of the enceinte alone when there are no other outworks; but, in the contrary case, also envelops the ditches of these, forming thus a continuous covered line of communication around the fortification.

The covering embankment itself is arranged towards the covered-way like an ordinary parapet, and it receives on the exterior a gentle slope or glacis.

By this arrangement the garrison have a covered position beyond the ditch where they can assemble with safety, either for the purpose of making a sortie, or to guard the ditches and the communications across them; and which affords them also a secure point of retreat if repulsed in a sortie, as a reserve left in the covered-way will be at hand to check the pursuit by their fire, and enable the retreating party to gain the enceinte.

**48. Places-of-Arms.** The covered-way, from the direction given to the counterscarps of the enceinte and outworks, forms a line of communication with salient and reëntering parts, Pls. 8, 9, Figs. 80 to 85.

The salient portions, s, are termed *salient places-of-arms;* and the reëntering parts the *reëntering places-of-arms.*

The salient places-of-arms, it will be seen, result from the general plan of the covered-way; but the reëntering places-of-arms are formed by changing the directions of the two branches where they form the reënterings, R, so as to make a salient within the reënterings; thus enlarging the covered-way at these points and producing a flanking arrangement, by which the glacis can be swept, and a cross-fire be brought to bear on the ground in advance of the salients.

**49. Traverses.** The covered-way, from its position and the usually slight command given to the crest of its glacis, is very much exposed to the effects of an enfilading fire.

With a view to remedy this defect, and also to enable the garrison to dispute foot by foot the possession of this outwork by the assailant, earthen masks, formed like an ordinary parapet and termed *traverses*, are thrown up across it. The traverses usually extend to the counterscarp, the wall of which is built up to sustain them.

At the end, towards the glacis, a passage, or defile, is left between them and the covering embankment, to admit of a free communication throughout the covered-way.

**50. Tenaille.** The Tenaille is a low work placed in the reëntering formed in the enceinte ditch by the curtain and flanks of the bastioned system, being isolated by a ditch between it and these parts of the enceinte. Its chief purpose is to serve as a mask, covering the scarp walls of this reëntering from fire, as well as the outlets to the enceinte ditch, which are usually placed in the centre of the curtains.

The tenaille has received various forms from engineers. In some cases it has been made with two faces or wings, making a reëntering angle opposite the centre of the enceinte curtain. In others the two wings, instead of being prolonged until they meet, are connected by a short curtain parallel to that of the enceinte. In some examples it has the form of a small bastioned front. In others it consists of two flanks connected by a curtain. These flanks in some cases have been casemated for guns and mortars. The tenaille is usually revetted with masonry both in front and rear. In some cases the ends alone, towards the flanks of the enceinte, are revetted, the intermediate portions consisting of an ordinary earthen parapet without either scarp or gorge wall.

**51. Demi-lune.** The demi-lune, Pl. 9, Figs. 81, 82, 83, 84, is a work in the form of a redan, D, placed in front of the enceinte curtain, which it masks from fire, as well as a portion of each face of the enceinte, at the shoulder angles of the bastions. It is isolated from the enceinte by the main ditch. From its importance the scarp and gorge of the demi-lune are generally revetted, though in some cases the revetment has been omitted.

**52. Counterguard.** The counterguard is an isolated work, C, Fig. 80, in the form of a redan, which envelops the faces of a bastion. In some cases it consists simply of an earthen mask having the profile of an ordinary parapet; but it is usually revetted both in front and rear.

**53. Redoubts.** The term redoubt, or *réduit*, is applied to outworks placed within other outworks; their object being to strengthen the defence of the principal work.

A work of this class is usually placed within the demi-lune, and is termed the *demi-lune redoubt.* Small works of this kind are also placed in the salient and reëntering places-of-arms of the covered-way, and are termed the *redoubt of the salient, or reëntering place-of arms.* These redoubts are in some cases simple earthen works; in others they are revetted; and in others casemated both for the service of artillery and small-arms.

**54. Tenaillon.** The term tenaillon, Pl. 9, Fig. 81, is applied to a kind of face cover, or counterguard, T, of the demi-lune. It is only to be met with in some of the old fortified places of Europe, and was added to give more strength to fronts where the demi-lune was too small.

**55. Horn-Work.** The horn-work, Pl. 9, Fig. 82, usually consists of a bastioned front, H, with the ordinary outworks, having two long branches, FF, or wings, which rest upon two adjacent bastions, or two adjacent demi-lunes, DD, of the enceinte; its covered-way forming with that of the enceinte a continuous line of communication. The object of this outwork is to strengthen a salient or other weak portion of the enceinte.

**56. Crown-Work.** The crown-work, Pl. 9, Fig. 83, consists of two or more bastioned fronts, C, with their outworks, placed in front of some portion of the enceinte, to give it additional strength. It is terminated like the horn-work by two wings, FF, which rest either upon the enceinte, or upon two demi-lunes, DD. Its covered-way, like that of the horn-work, forms a continuous communication with that of the enceinte.

## VIII.

### ADVANCED AND DETACHED WORKS.

**57.** The term *advanced works* is applied to such works as, placed beyond the outworks, are still in defensive relations with them and the enceinte, by being so brought under the fire of either the enceinte or the outworks that the ground in advance of them will be well swept by this fire; their ditches flanked by it; and their interior so exposed to it that, if the work were seized by an open assault, the assailant could be driven from it by this fire.

*Detached works* are those which, although having an important bearing on the defence of the main work, are so far from it as to have to depend solely on their own strength in case of assault.

Advanced works are usually in the form of redans or lunettes, and in some cases horn and crown works, depending on the extent of ground that it may be thought necessary to occupy with them.

Detached works depending solely on their own strength, should have a revetted scarp and counterscarp of sufficient height to present great difficulties to an open assault, and have their ditches flanked either from the parapet of the work itself, or by caponnières, or by counterscarp galleries.

**58.** Advanced works are placed in positions which the assailant must necessarily make himself master of before he can approach nearer to the main work; or on points which overlook ground that cannot be swept by the fire of the enceinte; and sometimes on points which, inaccessible to the assailant, give good position from which a flank fire can be brought to bear upon ground over which the assailant will be obliged to make his approaches.

Restricted to these purposes, an advanced work may be of great value in prolonging the defence; and every precaution should be taken to secure the work from a surprise, and to give its garrison a safe means of communication with the outworks upon which they can retire when forced to abandon their work.

In works of great extent, with full and strong garrisons, advanced works, by judicious combination with the works in their rear, may greatly enlarge the field of action of the garrison; keeping the assailant at a distance and annoying him by frequent sorties in large bodies, made under the protection of the outworks.

**59.** Detached works may be either of a polygonal or bastioned form, depending upon the extent of ground to be occupied; the former being more suitable to small works to which the bastioned form does not lend itself.

They belong to the class of works termed *forts*, as distinguished from fortresses. Their principal use is to occupy ground like commanding heights, which, although not within good sweep of the fire of the main work, is still within range of the heaviest calibres of the assailant, and which if occupied by him would prove a source of serious annoyance to the work.

The more favorite mode now among engineers for the defensive works of cities, is to inclose them with a continuous enceinte of sufficient strength to repel an open assault, and to occupy positions in advance of the main works by forts which will force an assailant to take up ground too far off to reach the main defences by his fire, and to oblige him to get possession of one or more of these forts by a regular siege to enable him to approach the main work.

In Pl. 9, Fig. 84, is an advanced work, L, flanked by the demi-lunes, D, of the enceinte. The plan of this work is a lunette with its covered-way and places-of-arms, R and S.

## IX.

### INTERIOR RETRENCHMENTS.

**60.** Besides the works exterior to the enceinte, the object of which is to retard the assailant in his attempts to enter it by breaching, engineers have placed within it other works which, in some cases, are designed simply to enable the garrison to make an effectual defence of the breach, when the assault upon it is made, and give them a secure point of retreat and safety when driven from it; and in others these interior works are chiefly designed to bring plunging fire to bear on the assailant's siege works exterior to the enceinte. The former class, intended for the defence of the breach alone, are termed *interior retrenchments;* and the latter *cavaliers.*

**61.** Interior retrenchments are either placed within the bastions, which are the parts of the enceinte usually breached, or in rear of their gorges. Those which are placed within the bastions, extend across them either between the faces or between the flanks. When placed at the gorge they connect the two adjacent curtains.

The plan of these works varies with their position, the size of the bastions, or the more or less openness of their salient angles.

In small bastions with acute salients, when the retrenchment rests upon the faces, it usually receives the form of a tenaille or inverted redan, the angle of the tenaille being about 100°. When the bastions are large and the salient angle quite open or obtuse, the retrenchment may receive the form of a small bastion front, Pl. 9, Fig. 85, resting upon the faces.

Either of these forms may in like manner be used, when the retrenchment rests upon the flanks of the bastion. But as this position enables a retrenchment of the form of an ordinary redan to have its ditches swept by the fire of the flanks of the adjacent bastions, this form is in some cases used in preference.

When placed between two curtains at the gorge of a bastion the plan of the retrenchment is always a bastioned front.

**62.** Cavaliers are placed either upon the curtains or within the bastions. The latter is the more usual position selected for them. Their plan in this position is usually that of a lunette, the faces and flanks of which are parallel to those of the enveloping bastion. Cavaliers receive a considerable command over the parapet of the enceinte, and, in some cases, they are arranged with a tier of casemated fire, above which is an open battery.

Interior retrenchments and cavaliers are usually constructed with a revetted scarp and counterscarp to secure them from an open assault; and, in some cases, a covered-way, with a small reëntering place-of-arms, R, Pl. 9, Fig. 85, closed by traverses, is arranged in advance of the ditch, to insure the safe retreat of the garrison when driven from the breach.

# CHAPTER II.

## SYSTEMS OF FORTIFICATION.

### SUMMMARY.

Description and analysis of the bastioned system (Art. 63).—Methods of Vauban (Art. 65).—Description of Vauban's 1st Method (Art. 66).—Description and analysis of Cormontaigne's Method (Art. 77).—Method of the schools of Mézières and Metz (Art. 162).—Noizet's Method (Art. 99).—Choumara's Method (Art. 95).

## I.

### BASTIONED SYSTEM.

**63.** A bastioned enceinte consists of a series of bastions which occupy the salient angles of the polygon within which the enceinte is inclosed; the flanks of the bastions being usually connected by straight curtains.

The sides of the polygon which connect the salient angles of the bastions are termed the *exterior sides*, in contradistinction to the sides of an interior polygon which, being parallel to the first and occupying the positions of the curtains, are termed the *interior sides*.

The bastioned enceinte, when its relief and plan are suitably arranged, possesses the advantages of having its ditches thoroughly swept from within the enceinte itself, thus securing the flanking arrangement of the scarp; of bringing a cross and flank fire to bear upon the approaches on the salients of the enceinte, and furnishing a strong direct and cross fire upon the site in advance of the curtains and the faces of the bastions.

**64.** The principal objections urged against the bastioned system are:

1. That its chief characteristic, a perfect flanking disposition for the entire line of the scarp, is attainable only under certain relations between the requisite relief for a permanent work and the lengths of the exterior side and curtain, which

therefore restricts it in its application to fortifications of a permanent character.

2. That, in order to secure a sufficient length of flank for an effective flanking disposition, the angle between the face of the bastion and the exterior side, termed the *diminished angle* of the polygon, has to be made so great as to decrease considerably the space inclosed within the polygon, whilst the development of the line of the enceinte is greatly increased by it.

3. That the direction necessarily given to the faces from this cause throws their prolongations in positions very favorable to the erection of enfilading batteries against them.

4. That the flanks, upon which the whole system is based, lie in positions in which, like the faces, they can be not only easily enfiladed but are further exposed to a reverse fire, from shot which may pass over the parapet of the faces as well as the opposite flank.

5. And that these objections are the stronger as the salient angles of the polygon are smaller or as the number of sides is decreased.

Besides these objections, which to a certain extent are well founded, where the defensive arrangements are chiefly open, as is the case in most land fronts, others have been urged against this system which, being rather of a comparative character, as showing the advantages of other systems over this, will best be examined elsewhere.

## II.

### VAUBAN'S FIRST METHOD.

65. Vauban has left examples of three different methods in the places planned by him. The fortress of New Brisac is fortified after his third method; those of Landau and Befort after his second; but the greater part of the places fortified by him are planned according to his first or earliest method.

66. **Profile of Enceinte.** In the profile of this method, Fig. 1, Pl. I., the scarp wall is 36 feet high, its slope being five perpendicular to one of base; surmounting this is another wall from 4 to 6 feet high, the object of which is to sustain the exterior of the parapet. The parapet is 18 feet thick, the superior slope being $\frac{1}{9}$; the interior crest is 8

feet above the terre-plein, which is 42 feet in width. The mean command of the interior crest above the site is about 26 feet. The bottom of the ditch is about 17½ feet below the site.

**67. Plan of Enceinte.** Vauban adopted no arbitrary or invariable combination of parts in his methods. His great excellence as an engineer is shown in the skill with which he adapted the fortifications he planned to the defensive requirements of the sites; selecting long, medium, or short exterior sides, and varying the lengths and directions of the faces and flanks so as to procure the best command over the exterior ground, and to withdraw these parts from the enfilading fire of the assailant.

In his works, however, he has generally taken 360 yards as the greatest limit of the exterior side; the perpendicular of the front ⅛ when the polygon is a square; ⅐ for the pentagon; and ⅙ for all higher polygons.

With these starting-points he procured diminished angles which gave more than 60° to the salient angles of the bastions in all cases, and flanks of suitable length both to flank the main ditch and to encounter with advantage the counter batteries which could be erected against them.

The following constructions both for the enceinte and outworks are taken from the best French authorities as adopted by him for polygons higher than the pentagon.

68. In the plan or tracè (Fig. 2, Pl. I.), the magistral is taken as the directing line; the exterior side is 360 yards; on the perpendicular of the front a distance of ⅙ the exterior side is set off; lines drawn through this point and the extremities of the exterior side, determine the directions of the faces, and the lines of defence; from the salients a distance equal to ²⁄₇ of the exterior side is set off, which gives the lengths of the faces and the positions of the shoulder angles; the flank is drawn by taking the opposite shoulder angle as a centre, and with a radius equal to the distance between the shoulder angles describing an arc to intersect the line of defence; the chord of this arc is the flank; the curtain is drawn by joining the extremities of the flanks. By this construction the flanks will be about 54 yards; the curtain, 146; and the lines of defence, 267; the length of these being determined so that the salients of the bastions can be defended with the *rampart gun*, or *wall-piece*.

**69. Tenaille.** In many of the places constructed before Vauban's time there was a *fausse-braie*, enveloping the enceinte and connected with it. This work was suppressed by Vauban, who was the first to use the tenaille in its place.

The tenaille is separated from the curtain by a ditch 10 yards wide, and from the flanks by ditches of 6 yards.

The form of the tenaille as used by Vauban was variable. In some cases he made it with a curtain and two small flanks parallel to those of the enceinte; in others it consisted simply of two wings placed on the prolongations of the faces; and finally, he gave it the form in Fig. 2, with a small curtain and two wings, which is the one at present most generally adopted. The relief of the tenaille is so arranged as not to mask the fire of the flanks on the ditch of the enceinte along the faces; for this purpose Vauban places its interior crest on a level with the site, or a little below it.

The tenaille has many valuable properties; it covers the postern under the curtain; masks the masonry of the curtain and flanks, so that a breach cannot be made in them, and in this way prevents retrenchments, resting against those parts, from being turned; a place-of-arms is formed between it and the curtain, where troops can be assembled for sorties in the ditches; finally, its fire sweeps the ditch and counterscarp, and helps to cover the retreat of troops from the other outworks.

**70. Main Ditch.** Vauban followed no invariable rule in regulating the dimensions of the enceinte ditch; its most usual width at the salients of the bastions, where the counterscarp is an arc of a circle, is about 36 yards; the rest of the counterscarp is tangent to this arc, and directed upon the opposite shoulder angles.

**71. Demi-lune and Rêduit.** Vauban increased the dimensions of the demi-lune, which had been used previous to his time.

The object of this work is to secure the gates of the place from a surprise; to mask from the enemy's batteries the flanks and curtain of the enceinte; to give cross-fires on the salients of the bastions, and to favor sorties.

The plan and dimensions of the demi-lune vary also in Vauban's works. Its magistral is generally laid out by taking a point on the bastion face at 10 yards from the shoulder angle, and drawing a line from this point to the perpendicular of the front, so as to make the face of the demi-lune equal to $\frac{5}{7}$ of the exterior side. The parapet of the demi-lune is the same as that of the enceinte; its command is 3 feet less than that of the enceinte.

All the outworks in this system are commanded by the enceinte; the outworks most advanced being also commanded by those in rear.

The ditch of the demi-lune is generally about 24 yards wide, and of the same depth as that of the enceinte; its counterscarp and that of the enceinte forming a continuous wall.

**72.** To strengthen the demi-lune, and secure for the troops entrusted with its defence a safe retreat when it is carried, Vauban placed in it a small redoubt. This work, in some instances, was only a simple *loop-holed wall* with a ditch in front; sometimes it was made of earth, and after the commencement of the siege.

**73. Covered-way.** The covered-way envelops the entire counterscarp. The general width of the covered-way is 12 yards.

To set out the reëntering place-of-arms, two points are taken, at 20 yards from the reëntering angle, made by the interior crests of the covered-ways of the demi-lune and bastion, and upon these crests, and from these points as centres, with radii of 24 yards, arcs are described; the point of their intersection being joined with the centres gives the crests of the reëntering place-of-arms.

The parapet of the covered-way is terminated in a glacis, the foot of which is from 40 to 50 yards from the interior crests.

**74. Traverses.** To close the places-of-arms, and enable the troops to defend the covered-way foot by foot, traverses of earth formed into parapets are placed at the places-of-arms. Defiles or passages of 4 feet are left between the traverses and the crest of the covered-way, for the circulation of the troops. The covered-way is palisaded to prevent surprise.

Vauban placed a high value on this work, which, to use his own words, "costs less to the defence and more to the assault than any other work." The covered-way prevents all access to the ditch, by a strong fire of musketry, which sweeps all the exterior ground; it is a secure position where troops can be assembled in safety for sorties; it covers the retreat of troops from the exterior into the other works.

**75. Communications.** In Vauban's front, ramps are made to ascend from the plane of site to the terre-plein.

A postern is made under the curtain to communicate from the interior with the ditch; another postern is made under the tenaille to lead to the demi-lune. A *double caponnière*, which is a passage covered on each side by a parapet terminated in a glacis towards the ditch, covers the communication through the ditch to the gorge of the demi-lune. Single caponnières are placed in the ditch of the demi-lune, and cover the troops from the enemy's fire through its ditch.

Stairs are placed at the gorges of the tenaille and demi-lune, and along the counterscarp at the places-of-arms, to ascend from the ditch to the terre-pleins of those works.

To communicate with the exterior, narrow openings are made in the faces of the reëntering place-of-arms, to lead from the terre-plein to the glacis; they are termed *sortie-passages or sally-ports;* and are closed by barriers.

76. **Analysis.** In the *traçé* adopted by Vauban for the enceinte, it may be observed that the length and positions of the lines of the front, resulting from it, are in good defensive relations both for cannon and small-arms.

1. The foot of the scarp, throughout the length of the curtain and the bastions, is thoroughly swept by the fire of the flanks.

2. The length of the flank is sufficient to contain as many cannon at least as the assailant can place to counter-batter the flank from the glacis crest opposite the flank; and the flank can also bring an efficient fire of small-arms to bear on this battery of the assailant.

3. The bastions are capacious, and would admit of efficient interior retrenchments being thrown up in them, although Vauban does not indicate this auxiliary in his first method.

4. The tenaille was devised mainly to mask the scarp wall of the curtain and flanks, whilst its relief was so regulated as not to intercept the fire of the flanks on the enceinte ditch before the bastion faces.

The plan of the earlier tenailles consisted of two flanks connected by a curtain, which were parallel to the same lines of the enceinte. This form was subsequently abandoned, as the flanks were found to be exposed to both an enfilading and reverse fire, from the assailant's positions in front of the enceinte; and the one now in most general use, consisting of either two wings simply, or of two wings connected by a short curtain, adopted in its place.

The tenaille, however, only partially subserves its object, as it does not cover the entire height of the scarp of the enceinte curtain and flanks; and, what is a more serious defect, it leaves the entire height of scarp of that portion of the curtain, opposite to the ditch between the tenaille and the bastion flank, entirely exposed, from the same position, and liable to be breached.

5. From the small size of the demi-lune, it gives but little cover to any portion of the enceinte scarp except the curtain. It is not sufficiently thrown to the front to give a good volume of cross-fire on the glacis in advance of the bastion salients ; and the reëntering formed at this point, by the two adjacent demi-lunes, is, from the same cause, shallow and of but little strength. Owing to this last defect the assailant can easily breach and storm the enceinte at the same time as the demi-lune.

Besides these defects the demi-lune is not provided with a permanent réduit, a work necessary to enable the demi-lune to make a vigorous defence, by the support it affords the assailed.

6. From the width given to the demi-lune ditch, the covered-ways are exposed to a slant reverse fire, from which they are but badly screened by the traverses. Their command over the site is rather too little. Their main defect, however, is the small size given to the reëntering place-of-arms, and the failure to secure this important position for assembling troops for sorties by a permanent réduit, by which any open attack of the covered-way could be checked.

7. The dimensions given both to the enceinte and demi-lune ditches present a formidable obstacle to an open assault, and render the assailant's passage of the ditch by the sap also more difficult. The demi-lune ditch, however, offers a wide opening through which the scarp of the bastion-face can be seen down to its foot from the assailant's batteries on the glacis crest in the prolongation of the demi-lune ditch.

8. The communications within the enceinte, and from it to the main ditch, are sufficient and convenient for the character of the defence designed. Those of the outworks are for the most part narrow, inconvenient, and but badly screened from the assailant's fire, and therefore do not furnish a good provision for an active defence beyond the enceinte.

9. The great command over the site, and the high relief given to the enceinte, are very much in favor of the defence both as to the effect of the fire on the assailant's approaches and for security against an escalade. But in attaining these objects Vauban has left exposed to the assailant's distant fire a considerable portion of the scarp wall, which, being destroyed, would lay the enceinte open to a surprise.

## III.

### CORMONTAINGNE'S METHOD.

**77.** Cormontaingne, the immediate successor of Vauban, holds a place only second to this master of the art in the estimation of the engineers of the French school. Cormontaingne, who to superior abilities united a wide range of experience both in the construction and in the attack of permanent works, studied with great care the results of Vauban's immense labors. In planning the front which has received his name, Cormontaingne seems to have applied himself rather to remedy the defects noticeable in the methods of Vauban, than to produce any radical change in the combinations which had thus far received the sanction of engineers generally. He was thus led to reject the 2d and 3d methods of Vauban, and to take the 1st method as the basis of his own changes.

**78.** Cormontaingne was the first to develop clearly the influence of large demi-lunes on the progress of the attack, by their forming deep reënterings between them in front of the bastion salients; and also the increased strength gained by fortifying on a right line, or on polygons with a great number of sides, as in both of these cases the fronts assailed cannot be enveloped by the assailant's works, and the demi-lunes from their salient position intercept the prolongations of the bastion-faces, and thus mask them from the positions from which alone an enfilading fire could be brought upon them.

**79.** He likewise lays down as a principle that *no masonry should be exposed to the distant batteries of the assailant*, and to obtain this point he has so arranged the height of his principal scarps, and the command given to the glacis crest in front of them, that the top of the scarp shall not lie above the level of the crest, thus masking from view the entire scarp, by the earth forming the glacis, from all positions in advance of the glacis crest.

His modifications of the plan and profile of Vauban's 1st method, chiefly result from the above as a basis.

**80. Enceinte.** The modifications of Vauban's tracé (Fig. 4, Pl. I.) are different in the various works of Cormontaingne; but the following he indicates in his memoirs as the one preferred by him.

The exterior side is 360 yards; the perpendicular $\frac{1}{6}$; the faces of the bastions $\frac{1}{3}$ of the exterior side; the flanks are 40 yards, and are so placed that the curtain shall be 120 yards. This combination makes the lines of defence somewhat less, and the bastions larger than in Vauban's method.

The dimensions of the enceinte ditch are so regulated by Cormontaingne as to furnish earth sufficient for the embankments. It is 28 yards wide at the salient, and from 2 to 4 yards wider opposite the tenaille; this admits the entire fire of the flanks to sweep the ditch.

**81. Tenaille.** The tenaille is made with a curtain and wings; a ditch 10 yards wide being left between it, the curtain, and the flanks.

**82. Demi-lune.** Cormontaingne placed little value on small demi-lunes, as they form but slight and therefore weak reënterings before the bastions, and consequently retard but little the enemy's attack upon them; besides this, a small demi-lune covers but very imperfectly the shoulder angles of the bastions.

To remedy these defects, his demi-lune is so laid out that the prolongations of the magistrals of its faces will intersect the bastion-faces at 30 yards from the shoulder angles; the lengths of its faces being 120 yards.

The ditch of the demi-lune is 20 yards wide; its depth is the same as that of the enceinte. By thus enlarging the demi-lune, sufficient space is gained to place a strong réduit in its interior. The defence of the demi-lune may be made with more obstinacy from the support it receives from the réduit; and the enemy will be obliged to carry it before he can assault the breach he may have made in the bastion face, as this breach is seen in reverse by the fire of the flanks of this work.

**83. Demi-lune Réduit.** To circumscribe as much as practicable the space in the demi-lune which the enemy, after he gains it, requires for his works, the extremity of the demi-lune terre-plein, which is also the top of the counterscarp of the réduit, is drawn at 20 yards from the magistral of the face; the ditch of the réduit is 10 yards wide, and the magistral of its face is parallel with the counterscarp. By this arrangement the ditch is well flanked by the face of the bastion near the shoulder angle.

To lay out its flanks, the counterscarps of the enceinte are prolonged to intersect the perpendicular of the front; from this point of intersection a distance of 20 yds. is set off along each counterscarp; the two points thus obtained are joined by a right line, which is the gorge of the work: from the extremities of the gorge two lines are drawn parallel to the capital of the demi-lune, these lines limit the terre-plein of the flanks; the magistrals of the flanks are drawn parallel to and at 16 yards from the last lines.

**84. Covered-way, &c.** The general width of the covered-way is 10 yards. Cormontaingne enlarged considerably the reëntering place-of-arms, to which he added a réduit with a revetted scarp and counterscarp. The addition of this work is a great improvement upon the covered-way of Vauban, who indicates in his works small réduits of earth, or tambours of wood, for the same purpose.

Cormontaingne's réduit increases the strength of the covered-way; the troops assembled in the covered-way for sorties are secure under its fires; it sees in reverse, and protects any breach made in the face of the demi-lune; finally, it serves, in connexion with the extremity of the demi-lune, to cover the opening left between the flanks of the bastion and the wings of the tenaille, through which, if a breach was made in the curtain, the interior retrenchments, resting upon either the flanks or faces of the bastion, could be turned.

To lay out the interior crests of the reëntering place-of-arms, two points are taken on the counterscarps of the bastion and demi-lune at 54 yards from their point of intersection; from these points as centres, with radii of 60 yards, arcs are described, whose intersection joined with the centres gives the direction of the faces.

The magistral of its réduit is found by a similar construction; distances of 40 yards being set off along the counterscarps, and the faces being drawn from these points so as to be 36 yards long. The ditch of the réduit is 5 yards wide and 2½ yards deep.

Traverses are placed along the covered-way, to close the places-of-arms, defend the covered-way, and intercept projectiles fired in ricochet.

The crest of the glacis is broken into a cremaillère line, to allow room for the defiles of the traverses. The short branches of the cremaillère throw a fire on the salients of the covered-way; the positions of the long branches are so taken that the defiles may be seen and swept by the fire of the works in their rear.

**85. Profiles.** Cormontaingne, after a series of trials, whose object was to give the ditches such dimensions that they should furnish the earth required for the embankments, regulated the command of the different works as follows:

The lowest work, which is the demi-lune covered-way, he lays down as a rule, shall command the exterior ground by not less than 7½ feet; and the works most advanced shall be commanded by those in the rear.

It was found that, for the purpose of equalizing the excavations and embankments of the front, the crest of the demi-lune covered-way should have a command of 10½ feet above the natural ground.

The crest of the bastion covered-way, and of the reëntering place-of-arms, commands the crest of the demi-lune covered-way by 2 feet.

The magistral of the enceinte is horizontal, its elevation being the same as the mean elevation of the crest of the bastion covered-way.

The scarp wall is 30 feet high. This dimension has since been generally adopted by engineers, a wall of this height opposing a sufficient obstacle to an attempt at escalade.

The salient of the bastion commands its covered-way by 8 feet. The absolute relief of the flanks is 38½ feet. With this relief a piece, firing under a depression of $\frac{1}{6}$ through an embrasure in the flank, and in the direction of the curtain, will strike the bottom of the ditch at the middle point of the curtain; so that were the relief increased, the length of curtain remaining the same, the ditch would no longer be thoroughly flanked.

The relief of the tenaille is determined as in Vauban's method, so as not to mask the fire of the flanks upon the ditch opposite the extremity of the demi-lune; as it is here that a breach may be made in the bastion face, through the ditch of the demi-lune.

The demi-lune is commanded by the enceinte 3 feet, and by its own réduit 1½ feet. The demi-lune, therefore, commands its covered-way 7 feet, which is more than is indispensably requisite; for an enemy standing on the crest of the covered-way cannot have a plunging fire into a work in the rear of it, if the latter commands its crest by 5 feet.

The réduit of the reëntering place-of-arms commands the crest of the glacis only 4½ feet; its interior crest is so placed as not to mask the fire of the bastion faces on the glacis in advance of it.

The interior crests of all the works are 7½ feet above their terre-pleins, except that of the tenaille, which is 6½ feet; and of the réduit of the reëntering place-of-arms, which is 9 feet.

The interior crests of the faces of all the works exposed to enfilading fires are one foot higher at the salients than at the extremities.

The profile of the parapet of the principal outworks is the same as that of the enceinte.

**86. Communications.** The communications are generally of the same nature, and placed about in the same positions as in Vauban's method.

**87. Glacis.** The planes of the glacis are so determined that they may be swept by the fire of the works in the rear; their inclination is usually about twenty-four base to one altitude.

**Interior Retrenchments.** Cormontaingne indicates the gorge and shoulders of the bastion as the position for an interior retrenchment, when this addition to the front is made solely with a view of disputing the breach in the bastion and its interior with the assailant. In this case he gives the retrenchment the form of a tenaille, or a bastioned front, resting it either upon the shoulder angles of the bastion, or upon the two adjacent curtains on points beyond the prolongation of the ditch between the tenailles and the flanks, and in this position he gives it the form of a bastioned front.

In the former case, the portion of the interior of the bastions between the flanks is preserved for the defence, but the retrenchment is liable to be turned, by a breach made in the flank, or in the portion of the curtain where it joins the flank. In the latter case a breach in the bastion places the whole of the interior within view of the assailant, but the retrenchment itself is secure, from its position, from being turned, as a breach in the curtain cannot be made in rear of it.

**88. Cavalier.** When a greater command of the site than that afforded by the enceinte is requisite on any front, Cormontaingne places a cavalier within the bastion. To this work he gives the same form as that of the bastion; placing the faces and flanks of the two parallel to each other. The faces of the cavalier are alone revetted, as well as the counterscarp of their ditch, which is cut within the bastion. This ditch is broken off at the shoulder angles of the cavalier, and directed upon the faces; these portions also having a revetted scarp and counterscarp. A parapet is thrown up behind the scarp and between the flank of the cavalier and the bastion faces; thus isolating the anterior portion of the bastion, and furnishing an interior retrenchment which, when the shoulders and flanks of the bastions are masked from the assailant's view, can only be carried by a breach made either in the cavalier face, or in the portions resting on the cavalier and bastion faces.

**89. Analysis.** From the preceding description, it appears that the most important modifications made by Cormontaingne in Vauban's first method, consist:

1. In the means taken to cover the *masonry* from distant batteries.

2. In more capacious bastions susceptible of receiving efficient permanent interior retrenchments.

3. In an enlarged demi-lune, which places the bastions in strong reënterings, covers the shoulder angles, and admits of a réduit in its interior, which work strengthens the demi-lune, and sees in reverse the breach made in the bastion face.

4. In an enlarged reëntering place of-arms, containing a réduit which strengthens the entire covered-way, and covers the movement of the troops in sorties.

These modifications, although of great value, and constituting an important step in the art, still leave much to be desired; and engineers since Cormontaingne's time have sought to remedy the defects of his method, of which the following are the principal:

1. The enceinte has rather too slight a command, and is without any bomb-proof shelters.

2. The inclination of the superior slope of its parapet, which is $\frac{1}{6}$, is too small to have the ditches well flanked.

3. A breach can be made in the bastion face through the ditch of the demi-lune.

4. There are dead spaces in the ditch of the demi-lune, near the extremities of its faces.

5. The rëduit of the reëntering place-of-arms is not tenable after the demi-lune is taken.

6. The traverses of the covered-way do not afford the requisite protection to that work.

7. Finally, the communications are mostly inconvenient, and not well covered from the assailant's fires.

**90. Counterguard.** Vauban, in his third method, forms his enceinte with a high scarp wall, of the same dimensions and form as in his first method; and he procures his flanking arrangements for the enceinte by small bastioned towers of masonry, which are casemated in the lower story, and have an open battery in the upper, covered by a masonry parapet.

This enceinte he covers with spacious counterguards of the form of lunettes; the faces, flanks, and gorges of which are revetted, and which cover the bastioned towers of the enceinte; and between the flanks of these counterguards, and covering the curtain of the enceinte between the bastioned towers, he places a tenaille.

A demi-lune, in the form of a lunette, is placed in front of the counterguards and tenaille; within which he has placed a réduit with a revetted scarp and counterscarp. The whole of this combination of outworks he incloses with a covered-way arranged in the usual manner.

**91.** Cormontaingne uses the counterguard only as an exceptional outwork; and has applied it, in some of the works constructed by him, to strengthen a point that would otherwise have been too weak; but not, as by Vauban, as a constituent part of his method.

**92.** Two of the most eminent modern engineers, Coehoorn and Carnot, in their methods, use earthen counterguards to cover their enceintes, giving them only sufficient thickness at the top for a parapet and a banquette for infantry; so that, being taken by the assailant, he will not find sufficient room to place a breach battery upon their terre-pleins against the enceinte. In this way they serve chiefly as masks or face covers to the enceinte faces.

**93.** Haxo forms of the counterguard a constituent element of his method, giving it, like Vauban, the form of a lunette.

**94.** Noizet, although adopting the features of Cormontaingne's method as the basis of his, speaks of the counterguard as a valuable, and sometimes a necessary, element of a front; preferring it in some cases to the demi-lune.

Like all other outworks, when used, it should be flanked by the enceinte flanks; be swept on the interior by the fire of its faces; and not intercept their fire on the ground in advance of it.

## IV.

### METHODS OF THE SCHOOLS OF MÉZIÈRES AND METZ.

**95.** The School of Application for engineer and artillery officers, first established at Mézières and subsequently at Metz, has given to France, from about the period of the French Revolution down to the present day, the far greater portion of the many able officers who have gained such universal and deserved celebrity for these two corps.

In these schools the precepts of Vauban and Cormontaingne have been jealously regarded as the highest authority, and their manuscripts and published works have formed the basis of the instruction given in them.

**96.** Some slight modifications were proposed in the front of Cormontaingne by two engineers, *Chatillon* and *Duvigneau,* and taught by them in the course of permanent fortification given in the school. These changes chiefly consisted in enlarging the demi-lune and making it more salient; and in placing in the flanks of its reduit casemates for cannon with reverse views on the breaches that might be made in the bastion faces.

**97.** The teaching of the school of Metz has received its principal impress from General Noizet, himself a pupil of General Haxo, regarded as the first among the successors of Vauban and Cormontaingne, who for several years, whilst a captain of engineers, performed the functions of professor of fortification, and who has recently given to the public the results of his lectures delivered in the school.

**98.** The front which, for some years back and up to the present time, has been taught in this school, goes by the appellation of *Noizet's Method.* In it there is no sensible departure from the views and methods of Vauban and Cormontaingne; the object being to introduce such modifications into the front of the latter as would remedy some of its acknowledged defects.

In doing this, another object was kept in view which was to present, in the combinations of this front, a problem, in the solution of which the pupil would be called upon to apply both the elementary principles of fortifications and the geometrical methods that the engineer has to use as his principal tool in such problems, to a special case, that of a front adapted to a *horizontal site.* It is in this point of view that the analysis and construction of this front have been adopted as the basis for the elementary instruction given in permanent fortification in this Institution.

## V.

### NOIZET'S METHOD.

**99. General Requirements.** Noizet in his front takes as the basis of the construction of the enceinte the length of the exterior side, and the command; assuming these within the limits laid down by Vauban and Cormontaingne; and in the combinations of outworks with the enceinte following the latter engineer; introducing only such modifications as seem to best fulfil the general conditions of the problem.

**100. General data of the Enceinte.** In the following description and analysis of the front of Noizet, the plane of comparison is assumed at 60 feet below the horizontal plane of site, the reference of which will be therefore (60.0). The yard is taken as the unit for the horizontal dimensions of the plan; and the foot as the unit for the references and vertical dimensions.

Converting the French measures into their equivalent English units, the exterior side of the front is 380 yards; the height of the scarp wall 33 feet; the command of the interior crest of the curtain over the plane of site 21 feet; and its height above the magistral 13 feet.

The dimensions of the exterior side and of the relief, as here given, are so taken as to secure an efficient flanking arrangement of the curtain; and of the outworks by the bastion faces.

**101. Profile of Enceinte.** (Pl. II., Fig. 4.) The profile of the enceinte here given is similar to that of Cormontaingne, and was adopted by subsequent engineers until the more recently modified one already described.

Its slopes and dimensions are as follows:—The scarp and counterscarp slopes $\frac{20}{1}$, or one base to twenty altitude. Exterior slope $\frac{1}{1}$, or 45°. Superior slope $\frac{1}{6}$. Interior slope $\frac{3}{1}$. Banquette slope $\frac{1}{2}$. Rampart slope $\frac{2}{3}$. Terre-pleins 8 feet below the interior crests. Berm 2 feet. Distance between the magistral and foot of the exterior slope 1.5 feet. Thickness of parapet 20 feet. Height of interior crest above the banquette tread 4.5 feet. General width of terre-plein estimated from the vertical through the interior crest 48 feet.

**102. Magistral of the Curtain.** The length of this is

determined by the condition that the artillery fire from the flanks, under the depression of $\frac{1}{6}$, shall attain a point at 1.5 foot above the bottom of the ditch at the centre of the curtain; the bottom of the ditch itself at the centre being, for the purposes of drainage, 1.5 foot higher than at the extremities of the curtain, thus giving to the scarp a height of 31.50 feet at the centre instead of 33 feet, the general height throughout the enceinte.

Supposing now a section (Pl. II., Figs. 2, 4,) to be made through the flank by a vertical plane passed through the foot of the curtain scarp, and that a line be drawn in it, parallel to the superior slope and at 3 feet below it, to represent the direction of the artillery fire, this line must attain the point at 1.5 feet above the bottom of the ditch at the centre of the curtain, to fulfil the required condition of a thorough flanking disposition throughout the entire extent of the enceinte. If, then, a horizontal line be drawn from the point to be attained to intersect the vertical through the interior crest, it will be the horizontal distance between the interior crest and the centre of the curtain, and, from the construction, will be equal to six times the perpendicular distance intercepted between it and the line of artillery fire.

Now, from the above there is given to calculate this base, the entire height of the interior crest above the bottom of the ditch 44.50 feet; the height of the same point above the line of artillery fire 3 feet; and the height of the point to be attained above the bottom of the ditch 1.5 feet. The distance sought, therefore, will be 6(44.50 feet — 4.50 feet) = 240 feet.

To obtain the length of the magistral corresponding to this distance, it will only be requisite to subtract from it the horizontal distance between the interior crest and the point of the section corresponding to the magistral of the flank.

This last distance is composed of the thickness of the parapet; the base of the exterior slope; and the berm. The first is 20 feet. The second is found by taking from the height of the interior crest above the magistral, which is 13 feet, one-sixth the thickness of the parapet, or 3.33 feet, which gives 13 feet — 3.33 feet = 9.66 feet. The third is 1.50 feet. The required distance, therefore, is 240 feet — (20 feet + 9.66 feet + 1.50 feet) = 208.84 feet, or 69.61 yards.

**103. Magistral of Enceinte.** (Pl. II., Fig. 5.) Having found the length of the magistral of the curtain, the projection of the magistral of the enceinte on the plane of reference is determined as follows:

Draw a line for the exterior side, and set off on it AB = 380 yards; bisect this distance by a perpendicular, on which set off CD = $\frac{1}{6}$ AB = 63.33 yards; from A and B draw lines through D, these are the directions of the faces and lines of defence; draw a parallel to CD on each side of it, and at 69.61 yards, the length of the half curtain, from it, join the points G and H where these parallels intersect the lines AD and BD prolonged; GH is the position of the curtain; GB and HA the lines of defence; from G and H draw a line making an angle $\frac{1}{6}$ with the perpendicular to the curtain at each of these points; the parts GE and FH of these last lines are the flanks, and AE and BF the faces.

The position of the magistral with respect to the plane of reference is determined as follows:

The magistral of the curtain is horizontal. As it is 13 feet below the interior crest, and this line is placed at 21 feet above the plane of site, the magistral is 8 feet above this plane, and therefore, from the position given the plane of comparison, 68 feet above this last plane; its reference, therefore, is (68.0). The flank is 1.5 feet lower at the shoulder than at the curtain angle, the reference of the shoulder is then (66.50). The face is horizontal, and its reference also (66.50).

**104. Manner of determining the position of a point of the Interior Crest.** To determine the projection of a point of the interior crest contained in a profile plane, the height of the point above the magistral being known; we first subtract from this height $\frac{1}{6}$ the thickness of the parapet, the remainder will be the height of the exterior crest above the magistral, and, when the exterior slope is $\frac{1}{1}$, will also be the base of the slope; adding together the thickness of the parapet, the base of the exterior slope as just determined, and the distance from the foot of the exterior slope to the magistral, the sum will be the horizontal distance between the magistral and interior crest, or the distance to be set off, along the trace of the profile plane, from the magistral, to obtain the projection of the required point of the interior crest.

**105. Interior Crest of the Enceinte.** (Pl. II., Fig. 6.) The position of the interior crest above the magistral is fixed as follows. That of the curtain is parallel to the magistral and 13 feet above it. Those of the flanks and faces of the bastion are contained in the same plane, the scale of declivity of which is taken parallel to the bastion capital. The position of this plane is determined by placing its horizontal, which coincides with a pan-coupé 4.30 yards in length at the bastion salient, at 4.50 feet above the horizontal drawn through the points where the flanks join the curtain.

The reference of the interior crest of the curtain from the above data will, therefore, be (81.0); and the horizontal distance of any point of it from the magistral 31.16 feet, or 10.38 yards, as these two lines are parallel.

Having drawn the projection of the interior crest of the curtain, the point where it joins the flank may be determined approximately, and with sufficient accuracy, by bisecting the curtain angle of the magistrals, and taking the point where the bisecting line cuts the interior crest as the extremity of the flank. From this point, of which the reference is (81.0), if a line be drawn perpendicular to the bastion capital it will be the horizontal (81.0) of the plane of the interior crests of the bastion; that at the pan-coupé is 4.50 feet higher, and its reference will, therefore, be (85.50).

To find the position of this last horizontal, which is also that of the pan-coupé, draw two lines parallel to the bastion capital and 2.15 yards from it; they will limit the pan-coupé. Now, as the extremity of the pan-coupé is a point of the interior crest of the bastion face, and its reference is (85.50), the height of this point above the magistral is 19 feet, as the reference of this last line is (66.50). The horizontal distance, therefore, from this point to the magistral is (20 feet + 15.66 feet + 1.50 feet) = 37.16 feet = 12.38 yards. Drawing a parallel, therefore, to the magistral of the face and at 12.38 yards from it, the point where it cuts the parallel to the capital, at 2.15 yards from it, will be the required point, through which the horizontal (85.50) is drawn.

Having two horizontals of the plane, its scale of declivity can be constructed, and other horizontals be determined. The projection of the point of the interior crest of the face on any given horizontal can be found by the same process as the one just described. For example, take the horizontal (84.0); the perpendicular distance of the point on it from the magistral is (20 feet + 14.16 feet + 1.50 feet) = 35.66 feet, or 11.88 yards. The two points thus determined, being joined, will give the projection of the interior crest of the face.

To find that of the flank, of which one point (81.0) has been found, bisect the shoulder angle of the magistral, the point where the bisecting line cuts the interior crest of the face will give approximately the other extremity of the line required.

**106. Remark.** The constructions for the interior crests, just given, are only approximations to a true result; as the horizontal distances calculated, being thus contained in profile planes, ought to have been set off perpendicular to the projection of the interior crest; but the difference between the results of this approximate method and one rigorously accurate will, in the present case, be so small, owing to the slight divergence between the projections of the magistral and interior crest of the face, as not to affect, in any appreciable degree, the real positions of the required points. The same remarks are applicable to the constructions for finding the extremities of the flank.

**107. Parapet of Enceinte.** Having drawn the interior crest of the enceinte, all the other lines of the parapet—except the foot of the exterior slope—and the inward line of the terre-plein, are drawn parallel to it. The foot of the exterior slope is drawn parallel to the magistral.

**108. Terre-plein of Enceinte.** (Pl. II., Fig. 6.) The terre-pleins of the faces and flanks are in a plane parallel to that of their interior crest and 8 feet below it, estimated vertically. To find the reference of any horizontal of the terre-plein, it will be only necessary to subtract 8 feet from the corresponding one of the interior crests. Thus (85.50) being a reference of a horizontal of the interior crest, that of the terre-plein corresponding is (77.50).

The terre-plein of the curtain slopes 1 foot from the foot of the banquette slope to its inward line, which places this last 9 feet below the interior crest.

**109. Rampart Slope and Ramps.** (Pl. II., Fig. 6.) The rampart slopes are planes of $\frac{2}{3}$ passed through the inward lines of the terre-pleins. The lines of intersection of the rampart slopes and plane of site are found in the usual way.

The ramparts leading from the plane of site to the terre-plein receive an inclination of $\frac{1}{9}$, and they are 4.30 yards wide. Two of them are placed on the curtain; one on the flank; and one on the face.

**110. Analysis of Constructions adopted for the Enceinte.** Noizet, in the plan of his enceinte, has adopted dimensions and constructions which give results, for the most part, the same as those of Vauban and Cormontaingne, making the defensive properties of these different methods about equal.

The extent of the exterior side, the length of the curtain, the diminished angle, and the direction assumed for the flanks, produce a combination giving an efficient flanking, both as to direction and amount of fire, for the entire scarp, and a powerful cross-fire upon the covered-way and its glacis in advance of the bastion salient.

The lines of defence, by this combination, being within the effective range of small-arms, and the flanks capable of receiving a battery superior to the counter batteries that can be brought against them from the glacis crest of the opposite covered-way.

The dimensions and form of the profile are those usually adopted for permanent works, where the embankments are formed of ordinary earth, and the revetment walls of good masonry.

They are such as experience has shown will give durability and stability to the masonry, from the pressure of the embankments, and the ordinary causes of destructibility to which it is liable when exposed to the weather; and to the rampart and parapet the strength to resist the action of the heaviest artillery, whilst they offer to the assailed every convenience for their prompt action, and the use of their arms.

The width and slopes of the ramps are regulated for the passage of artillery. Where the height to be overcome is slight, as that between the terre-plein and barbette, the slope of the ramp may be as great as $\frac{1}{6}$, and its width be 3.30 yards. Where the height is greater, the declivity of the ramp should be proportionally less steep, and its width be 4.30 yards at least.

The position of the terre-plein with respect to the interior crests is that usually considered necessary to give shelter to the troops and *materiel* on it.

By inclining that of the bastion, the *materiel* and *personnel* on the faces and flanks are better covered from the enfilading and ricochet fire than they would be if the terre-plein was horizontal; as a ball passing over the salient will reach an inclined terre-plein at a point farther from the salient than one which is horizontal.

The height, 4.50 feet, at which the salient is placed above the curtain, is as great as can be admitted in a hexagon, the least polygon to which the traçé adopted is applicable;

because, if placed higher, the plane of the interior crest of the bastion, prolonged back, would intersect the plane of site in a line which would fall without the salients of the two adjacent bastions of the polygon, and these bastions would therefore not cover the one between them from reverse fire.

The slopes moreover of the terre-pleins keep them in a serviceable state, by not allowing the rain-water to collect and remain upon them.

**111. Particular Conditions of the Outworks.** The outworks, besides satisfying the general conditions already laid down, are connected with each other by several minor relations of defence and suitableness, growing out of their relative positions, which give rise to many seemingly arbitrary constructions and details for each one, the bearing of which cannot be clearly explained until a description of the whole as a system has been gone into.

The scarp walls of outworks, as well as their gorges where they are exposed to be turned, should not be less than 12 feet high to secure them from a sudden open assault.

Their parapets are of the same form as that of the enceinte; and for the more important ones, which are much exposed to the artillery of the assailant, of the same dimensions. In those less exposed, the thickness of the parapet may be reduced to 12 feet, or 4 yards.

The terre-pleins of the smaller outworks, which are not habitually armed with artillery, should not be less than 8 yards wide; those of the larger should not be less than 10 yards.

The banquette treads of outworks, like the caponnières and covered-ways, require a palisading for their greater security from assault, should be 6 feet wide.

**112. Tenaille.** (Pl. III., Figs. 1, 2.) The form of the tenaille is that of Cormontaingne's front; the magistral of its curtain being parallel to that of the curtain of the enceinte, and the scarp of its wings on the prolongation of the scarp of the bastion-faces.

A ditch of 13 yards is left between the gorge of the tenaille and the enceinte curtain; and one of 11 yards between each of its wings and the flanks. The magistral of its curtain is horizontal, and 13 feet above the crests of the double caponnière. The magistral of each wing is a broken line, the lowest point of it being 13 feet above the bottom of the enceinte ditch. Its gorge and the extremities of its wings are revetted. Its interior crest is horizontal throughout, and 4.50 feet below the magistral of the enceinte curtain. The thickness of its parapet 12 feet. The width of the terre-plein at its curtain 8.66 yards. The parapet is terminated at the wings by traverses 12 feet thick, which extend from the interior crest to the scarp wall of the wings; the top of each traverse is on the same level as the interior crest. The traverses are terminated towards the parapet by planes of $\frac{1}{1}$.

To construct the principal lines of the tenaille from the preceding data, first draw a line parallel to the enceinte curtain, and 13 yards from it, for the gorge of the tenaille curtain; another line parallel to this, and at 8.66 yards, is the interior crest, of which the reference is (63.50), as it is 4.50 feet below the enceinte magistral at the curtain.

A level passage at 31.50 feet below the magistral of the enceinte curtain and at the reference (36.50), leads from the main ditch between the enceinte and tenaille, under this last work, and through a double caponnière in the main ditch in advance of it. The crests of the caponnière are 9 feet above the level of the passage and at the reference (45.50); and the magistral of the tenaille curtain is 13 feet above these crests and at the reference (58.50). The interior crest of the tenaille having the reference (63.50), is therefore 5 feet above its magistral. The horizontal distance then between the magistral and interior crest is $12+3+1.5=16.5$ feet or 5.50 yards; and as these lines are horizontal, their projections will be parallel and at this distance apart.

The interior crest and magistral of the wing will result from the following data. The scarp wall of the wing extends to the top of the traverse reference (63.50); its magistral then descends, from this level in the plane of $\frac{1}{1}$, which terminates this traverse, to a level of 13 feet above the bottom of the enceinte ditch, which being at this part 3 feet lower than the passage of the double caponnière, and at reference (38.50), will give (46.50) for the reference of the lowest point of the magistral of the wing; the reference of the point where it joins that of the curtain being as already determined (58.50).

To find then the lowest point of this magistral, draw a line 12 feet or 4 yards from the extremity of the wing, for the exterior line of the traverse; parallel to this line draw another at 17 feet = 5.66 yards, which is the base of the slope of $\frac{1}{1}$ that terminates the traverse; where this line cuts the line of defence is the required point. The horizontal distance between this point and the interior crest, calculated in the usual manner, is $12 + 15 + 1.50 = 28.50$ feet $= 9.50$ yards.

Describing from the point just found an arc with a radius 9.50 yards, and from the other extremity of the magistral another arc with a radius 5.50 yards, and drawing a tangent to these arcs, it will be the interior crest of the wings.

The gorge line of the wing is not drawn parallel to the interior crest, but determined as follows. From the point of intersection of the interior crests of the curtain and wings describe an arc with a radius 8.66 yards; from the point where the enceinte curtain magistral prolonged cuts the interior crest of the opposite flank, draw a line tangent to this arc, which will be the direction of the required line.

The gorge wall rises to the level of the terre-plein. That which terminates the wing is limited by the planes of the parapet, terre-plein, and top of the traverse, and is termed a *profile wall*, from the form of its outline.

**113. Analysis of Constructions, etc., of the Tenaille.** The tenaille is more important as a mask than as a defensive work. It covers the postern in the curtain, and also the masonry of the flanks and curtain from the enemy's batteries; which last is an essential point, if there are interior retrenchments resting either on the flanks, or curtain of the enceinte, as it will then be impracticable for an enemy to turn them, as he cannot make a breach in the enceinte behind the tenaille.

As a defensive work its fire bears upon the ditches, and their counterscarps, and it thus serves to cover the retreat of the troops from the other outworks.

When the ditches are dry, it is an indispensable part of the front, as the space in its rear forms a large place-of-arms where troops can be assembled to manœuvre against the enemy when in the ditches.

Vauban and Cormontaingne, we have seen, so fixed the relief of the tenaille as not to mask the fire of the flanks on the breach in the bastion. It is on this principle that Noizet has determined the position of its interior crest, and placed it at 4.50 feet below the magistral of the curtain.

In regulating its scarp wall, it is supposed that an enemy would attempt an assault from some point in the dead space in front of it; and its height is therefore arranged so that no part of it shall be less than 13 feet above any point that the enemy might there occupy.

The position given to its interior crest still leaves some portion of the masonry of the enceinte behind it exposed; but were the exposed part battered away, there would be still a formidable height of scarp left to the enceinte, the parapet of which also would be but slightly diminished in thickness by it.

The portion of the enceinte flank exposed, near the shoulder angle would be very considerable, were the exterior slope of the tenaille parapet extended to the extremity of the wing; it is to prevent this that a traverse is here placed.

The tenaille is seldom armed with cannon, although mortars are frequently placed in it; on this account *its terre-plein is reduced to* 8.66 *yards.*

Every part of the ditch between the tenaille and curtain should be swept by the flanks. It is to satisfy this condition that the gorge line of the wing is so drawn as to be seen by the piece that flanks the curtain of the enceinte.

The tenaille, although procuring decided advantages to the bastioned form, deprives it of one of its characteristic points, that of flanking every part of the ditch. For, in front of the tenaille, there is a dead space, where an assailant could assemble in safety to assault it. This defect, however, is of trifling magnitude, since were the tenaille taken, he could not establish himself in it; and the width given to the ditch, between it and the enceinte flank, is such as to preclude any attempt to escalade the enceinte from the top of the tenaille.

The terre-plein of the tenaille is inclined, for the purpose of defiling it from the enemy's establishment on the terre-plein of the demi-lune redoubt. The inclination of the plane of defilement depends on the arrangement of this redoubt.

**114. Double Caponnière.** (Pl. III., Figs. 1, 2.) The passage of the double caponnière is 3.30 yards wide at the bottom and on the same level as the bottom of the ditch at the middle of the curtain reference (36.50). The interior crests of this work are at 9 feet above the bottom of the passage; they are horizontal, and their reference (45.50). In the profile of the caponnière the base of the interior slope is 0.50 yards; the banquette is 2.0 yards wide; and the base of the banquette slope 3.0 yards; the horizontal distance then between the interior crest, and the foot of the banquette slope, is 5.50 yards, which being doubled, and added to 3.30 yards the width of the passage, gives 14.30 yards for the distance between the interior crests. The crests are drawn parallel to the perpendicular of the front, and limited by the curtain of the tenaille on one side, and a line drawn parallel to, and 3.30 yards within the exterior side on the other.

The embankment of the caponnière is terminated on the exterior by a glacis, which is prolonged to the bottom of the ditch. This glacis is determined, by passing a plane through the interior crest of the caponnière, and through the shoulder angle of the interior crest of the opposite bastion lowered three feet.

The caponnière is terminated towards the exterior side by a profile wall, along the line at 3.30 yards within the exterior side; this wall is prolonged from the exterior line of the banquette tread, to a point at 2.0 yards beyond the interior crest; at this point the direction of the wall is changed, so that, being prolonged, it may cut the interior crest of the enceinte flank, at a point 4.0 yards from the shoulder angle. The remaining part of the embankment on this side is terminated in a glacis, the plane of which is passed through the interior crest of the enceinte curtain, and through a line on the bottom of the main ditch at 4.0 yards within the exterior side. This plane intersects the first glacis in a line, a b, Pl. III., Fig 2, which is prolonged to its intersection, b, with a line, b c, on the first glacis, at 6.66 yards from the interior crest. A part of the first glacis is terminated at this line by a plane of $\frac{1}{1}$; the line of intersection of this plane of $\frac{1}{1}$ with the second glacis, is prolonged to intersect the line of the this wall directed on the flank, which gives the point where wall terminates.

As the bottom of the enceinte ditch has not yet been fixed throughout, its intersection with the first glacis still remains to be determined.

**115. Analysis of the Double Caponnière.** The caponnière serves both as a communication, and as a defensive work for the ditch. As the former, the passage should admit of a convenient circulation, without being too wide, which has determined its width at 3.30 yards. The interior crests should cover the troops within the caponnière from the enemy's establishments on the crest of the bastion covered-way; a relief 9 feet has been found sufficient for this purpose.

As a defensive work, its fire should sweep the ditch. It is for this purpose that its embankments are arranged on the interior as an ordinary parapet, and on the exterior in the form of a glacis. Its banquette tread is made 2.0 yards wide, as it should be palisaded.

In order that the embankment of the caponnière may not, by its relief, form dead spaces in the ditch, the plane of the first glacis is arranged so as to be swept by the artillery fire of the opposite flank. The plane of the second glacis, and the return wall, are so arranged as to be swept by the fire of the curtain, and of a part of the flank.

The portion of the first glacis, near the extremity, is made into a *glacis coupé*, leaving a sufficient thickness of parapet to cover the passage.

**116. Magistrals of Demi-lune Scarp and Counterscarp.** (Pl. III., Fig. 3.) To construct the magistral of the demi-lune, two points are taken on the exterior side at 103 yards from the perpendicular; through these points perpendiculars are drawn to the exterior side; the points where they cut the magistral of the bastion-faces are joined, and on this line an equilateral triangle is constructed; its sides will give the directions of the magistral of the demi-lune. The extremity, b, of the demi-lune face, is found by drawing a line at 11 yards, without the exterior side.

The counterscarp of the demi-lune is parallel to the scarp and at 18 yards.

**117. Counterscarp of the Enceinte.** (Pl. III., Fig. 3.) To construct the counterscarp of the enceinte, an arc is described from the salient of the bastion, with a radius of 26 yards; a perpendicular, b f, of 6.60 yards is drawn to the demi-lune face; if a tangent be now drawn to the arc, and a perpendicular be demitted from the point, f, on the tangent, their point of intersection, f′, should fall on the line drawn through the extremity of the double caponnière parallel to the exterior side. The point f′ is found, by constructing the curve which is the locus of the above conditions. The arc with the tangent drawn through f′ is the magistral of the counterscarp.

**118. Redoubt of the Re-entering Place-of-Arms.** (Pl. III., Fig. 3.) To determine the magistral of the redoubt of the reëntering place-of-arms; a line is drawn through the point, b, of the demi-lune face, and the extremity of the curtain, and prolonged beyond the demi-lune counterscarp. A point, a, is next taken on the perpendicular, at 5.0 yards from the demi-lune salient; and through this point and a point, c, assumed on the demi-lune counterscarp, an indefinite line is drawn. A line, c d, is next drawn, making an angle of 60° with the line, a c. Two lines, c′ d′, and c′ c″, are drawn, the first parallel to c d, and 4.30 yards from it; the second parallel to a c, and at 2.0 yards from it. If the point of intersection, c′, of these two lines falls on the line drawn through b, it will be the angular point of the redoubt; and the line c′ d′, the magistral of one of its faces. If the point, c′, does not fall on the line drawn through b, then a second point, c, must be chosen, and the same construction be again made. The different intersections, c′, will be points of a curve, which is the locus of the above conditions; and the intersection of this curve, with the line drawn through b, will give the required point. Having the face, c′ d′, the other face is determined as follows: a line is drawn parallel to the demi-lune counterscarp, and at 27.0 yards from it; a point is found on this line, and at 7.83 yards from c′ d′; from this point with a radius of 7.83 yards, an arc is described; a tangent drawn to this arc, from a point on the interior crest of the bastion-face, at 13 yards from the pan-coupé, is the direction of the required face, d′ d″, which is terminated at the bastion counterscarp.

**119.** (Pl. III., Fig. 3, and Pl. IV., Fig. 1). The ditch of the redoubt is horizontal; and the reference of its bottom is determined by supposing the plane of the superior slope of the bastion-face to be prolonged to the enceinte counterscarp; finding the reference of the point, d″, in this plane, and taking a point 4.50 feet below this, the reference thus found is (57.90). The scarp wall of the redoubt is 13 feet high; the reference of its magistral will therefore be (70.90).

The salient of the interior crest is 5.33 feet above the magistral; its reference is therefore (76.23), and its projection is evidently the point which we have already determined, at 7.83 yards from the magistral. The interior crest of the face, d′ d″, has a slope of two feet from the salient, to the extremity of this face, which condition fixes the extreme point of the interior crest at 7.16 yards from the magistral.

Having the interior crest of one face, that of the other, c′ d′, is found from the scale of declivity of the plane of the interior crest. This scale is drawn parallel to the bastion capital; and since we have already found two points of the interior crest, by referring them to this scale, we can, as in the case of the bastion, determine any required point of the other face.

A small flank of 6.0 yards is made perpendicular to the line, c′ c″, the line of the profile wall of the face c′ d′.

The terre-plein of the redoubt is 8.66 yards wide; its gorge is revetted with a wall 13 feet high.

**120. Analysis of the Redoubt, etc.** Having given the construction of the principal lines of the redoubt, we will now give the reasons in support of them.

We first observe, that on account of the ditch between the tenaille, and the enceinte flank, a breach might be opened in the curtain, by means of a battery, established on the glacis of the reëntering place-of-arms, if there was no mask between the ditch referred to and this glacis. By placing the angle, c, of the redoubt, on the line drawn through the extremity of the curtain, and the extremity b of the demi-lune, it is readily seen that these two works so combined cover the opening left by the ditch; since, it will be necessary to batter down either the angle, c′, or the angle, b, to unmask the curtain. The means here resorted to is of frequent use in fortification; and the problem may be thus stated: *a line being given, which is partially covered by an existing mass, from fires in a given direction, to interpose another mass, which combined with the first, shall entirely mask the given line.*

We have thus established that the point c′, shall be found on the line drawn through *b* and the extremity of the enceinte curtain.

The communication along the gorge of the redoubt to its ditch is by means of stairs, placed along the profile wall, c′ c″. The width of the stairs is 2.0 yards. The stairs, like all other communications, to be safe, must be covered from the enemy's fire. The point where the enemy can establish himself, to fire on the stairs, is along the crest of the demi-lune covered-way, around the salient place-of-arms. It is readily seen, from the position of the stairs and the demi-lune, that this work will partially cover the stairs; and, therefore, we shall only have to interpose some other mask, combined with it, to attain the object in view. The mask used is the point c, which is the angle of masonry formed by the counterscarp walls of the demi-lune and redoubt; the ditch of the redoubt being here 4.30 yards wide.

The position of the point a, through which the line a c is drawn, is so taken on the exterior slope of the demi-lune parapet, that the line of fire drawn through it will pass over a man's head, at the top of the stairs.

The angle c′, between the profile wall and face wall, is made 60°, as this is the minimum angle for masonry, to give it sufficient strength. The minimum is here taken to bring the face c′ d″, as far in as possible, and thereby make the reëntering as deep as the case will admit of.

The object of the redoubt is to strengthen the covered-way, and sweep with its fire the enemy's establishments on the glacis of the demi-lune. The principal works on this glacis are the breach and counter batteries, which occupy a space of about 17.0 yards, estimated from the crest of the glacis; if to this we add 10 yards, for the mean width of the covered-way, we obtain the distance 27.0 yards, which is the least distance that the salient of the redoubt can be from the counterscarp of the demi-lune, to sweep the entire flank of the batteries.

The direction given to the face d′ d″, is such as to allow of its being flanked by the bastion-face. The face is thrown out as far towards the salient of the bastion covered-way as possible, for the purpose of crowding the space along the crest of this covered-way, which the enemy requires for his batteries.

The redoubt being directly in front of the bastion-face, its relief should be reduced, that the fire of this face may not be too much masked. To effect this, we commence by establishing the bottom of its ditch, so that the point of it nearest the bastion may just be seen by the musketry fire of the face; we then adopt nearly a minimum relief of scarp wall; finally, we arrange the interior crest of one face, so as to allow no exterior slope at one extremity and make the other at the salient 2 feet higher. This slope of 2 feet and the direction given to the scale of declivity of the interior crest, determine a plane of defilement for the redoubt, the prolongation of which will pass at about 3 feet above the salients of the two demi-lunes, which are symmetrically situated with respect to the bastion capital. This is done in accordance with a principle generally adopted, that when one work is less advanced than another, and commanded by it, the plane of its interior crest prolonged should pass 3 feet above the points which the enemy can occupy on the advanced work—which from the nature of the attack must fall first into his possession—so that he may not have a plunging fire into the retired work, from his establishments, which are generally about 3 feet above the parapet of the work occupied.

The small flank of 6.0 yards perpendicular to the profile wall, is to obtain a reverse fire on the breach made in the demi-lune. The gorge of the redoubt is revetted to secure it from an assault.

**121. Demi-Lune Redoubt.** (Pl. III., Fig. 3, and Pl. IV., Figs. 1, 2.) The salient of the redoubt is 33.0 yards from the magistral of the demi-lune; finding a point on the perpendicular, at this distance from the magistral, we obtain the salient. The magistral of the face is found by drawing a line from this point, to the interior shoulder angle of the bastion.

To find the position of the interior crest of the face, the reference of the magistral must be given, and the scale of declivity of the plane of the interior crest. To determine the first, the salient of the demi-lune interior crest is placed at 3 feet below that of the enceinte curtain; this gives (78.0) for the reference of this point. The salient of the magistral of the redoubt is fixed at 8 feet below the salient of the demi-lune, which gives its reference (70.0). The magistral slopes from the salient towards the exterior side, and this slope is arranged, so that the point where the magistral cuts the exterior side shall be 5.70 feet, or 1.90 yards lower than the salient; the reference then of this point will be (64.30). Having thus two points of the magistral, its position is fixed.

To determine now the interior crest, a pan-coupé of 4.30 yards is made in the salient of the redoubt, and this commands the salient of the demi-lune by 1.5 feet. The reference then of the pan-coupé is (79.50). From the pan-coupé to the gorge of the redoubt, which is on the exterior side, the plane of the interior crest has a slope of 1.5 feet, and its scale of declivity is parallel to the perpendicular. To find the crest from the above data, it may be observed that the problem is similar to the one already solved in the case of the bastion; except, here the magistral being an inclined line, the distance of any one of its points, to the point on the interior crest, contained in a profile, is not known, since only one of the points is given. The following is the method, which applies to all similar cases, for doing this. It will be observed, that if the foot of the exterior slope be drawn, it will have the same slope as the magistral. Through the foot of the exterior slope then, which is known, the plane of the exterior slope whose inclination is $\frac{1}{1}$, is passed. If any horizontal line be now drawn in this plane, the horizontal distance between this line and a known point of the interior crest, contained in a profile, can be readily found.

To apply this to the case in point, first draw the foot of the exterior slope, which is 0.50 yards from the magistral; the reference of this line at the salient is (70.0), and at the gorge (64.30). To obtain the horizontal of the plane of the exterior slope whose reference is (70.0), describe from the point (64.30), an arc, with a radius 5.70 feet, or 1.90 yards; the tangent drawn to this arc, from the point (70.0) is the required line. The reference of the pan-coupé being (79.50), its distance from this horizontal line,—the thickness of the parapet being 20.0 feet,—is 26.17 feet, or 8.72 yards; and the reference of the interior crest at the gorge being (78.0), its distance from the same line is 8.22 yards; the two points thus found fix the position of the interior crest of the face.

The redoubt is made with flanks, the interior crests of which are parallel to the perpendicular, and 22.0 yards in length. To find the flanks, draw a line parallel to the exterior side, and at 22.0 yards; where this cuts the interior crests of the faces, will be the interior shoulder angles of the redoubt, from which the flanks are drawn parallel to the perpendicular.

The magistral of the flank is horizontal; its position is therefore easily found.

Joining the point, b, of the demi-lune, with the extremity of the interior crest of the flank; the direction of the wall which terminates the flank, the ditch of the redoubt, and the extremity of the demi-lune is found.

The terre-plein of the redoubt along the face is 8.66 yards wide; along the flank, the width is 11.0 yards. This terre-plein, which is eight feet below the plane of the interior crest, is called the *upper;* to distinguish it from the remaining interior space, called *the lower terre-plein*, and which is 13 feet below the upper. A portion of the upper terre-plein, for a length of about 14.0 yards from the extremity of the flank, is sustained by a wall of masonry. A portion of the interior space between the terre-pleins of the two flanks, for about 6.0 yards from the exterior side, is excavated to the bottom of the ditch.

The upper terre-plein, along the face, is connected with the lower by a slope of $\frac{2}{3}$. Two ramps 3.30 yards wide, with a slope of $\frac{1}{6}$, connect the two terre-pleins. The details of these constructions are best studied from Pl. IV., Fig. 1. The scarp wall of the redoubt is 16.50 feet high.

**122. Analysis, etc., of the Demi-lune Redoubt.** As the object of the demi-lune redoubt has been already explained, the reasons for the constructions employed in determining its dimensions, etc., only remain to be stated.

The redoubt should be as advanced as possible, to see in reverse the lodgments of the enemy on the glacis of the collateral works. To effect this, its salient is taken at 33.0

yards from the demi-lune magistral; this distance is sufficient to allow their proper dimensions to the parts of the demi-lune.

The face of the redoubt is directed on the interior shoulder angle of the bastion to have its ditch flanked by the bastion face.

In placing the salient of the magistral at 8 feet below the salient of the demi-lune, the top of the scarp wall will be nearly on the level with the demi-lune terre-plein. This arrangement will force an enemy, lodged on the demi-lune terre-plein, either to lower his battery to effect a breach in the redoubt, or else to employ a mine for this purpose; either of which operations will cost him much labor and loss of time.

The least command has been given to the redoubt over the demi-lune, to enable the fire of the redoubt to sweep the demi-lune terre-plein. This command of 1.50 feet, with the slope given to the plane of the interior crest, will prevent an enemy from having a plunging fire into the redoubt, from his lodgments in the demi-lune.

The flanks of the redoubt are principally to procure a reverse fire on the breach in the bastion faces; their length is estimated for 3 guns.

The piece nearest the extremity of one flank should be covered by the extremity of the opposite flank, from the reverse fire which might come through the redoubt gorge, from the enemy's lodgment on the bastion covered-way.

The terre-plein of the flank is made 11.0 yards, as it is habitually armed with cannon.

In the outworks, wherever it can conveniently be done, bomb-proof arches should be made, to serve as magazines, shelters, etc. This point has been effected in the redoubt, by the position given to the lower terre-plein; by this means sufficient space is gained under the flank for a bomb-proof shelter. The terre-plein of the flank is sustained by a wall, which is the interior facing of the shelter.

The scarp wall of the redoubt might have been reduced to the minimum dimension of 12 feet. But on account of its importance, and also not to diminish too much the interior space, it has been found that the dimensions adopted, 16.50 feet, best satisfy the requisite conditions. The top of the wall slopes towards the gorge, so that at the shoulder angle it may be about 4 feet lower than at the salient; the object of this is, to expose as small a portion of the wall as possible to the enemy's fire, through the demi-lune cut; which from its width, might admit of a breach being made in the redoubt, through it, from the enemy's lodgment on the reëntering place-of-arms. It will be seen further on, how the scarp of the redoubt is covered by the bottom of the cut.

**123. Demi-lune and its Cut.** (Pl. III., Fig. 3, and Pl. IV., Fig. 1.) To return now to the demi-lune and finish what relates to it, and the cut in its face.

To construct the scarp of the cut, the face, c′ d′, of the redoubt of the reëntering place-of-arms, is produced to intersect the magistral of the demi-lune; joining this point with the interior shoulder angle of the demi-lune redoubt, the magistral of the scarp is obtained.

The exterior width of the cut is found by setting off 6.60 yards on the demi-lune magistral, from the point where it is intersected by the face c′ d′. To obtain the interior width, an arc with the radius of 10 yards is described, from the exterior shoulder angle of the demi-lune redoubt; a tangent is drawn to this arc, parallel to the face of the redoubt; this tangent gives the direction of a wall, which limits the cut on the interior, and also the portion of the demi-lune, from the cut to the extremity of the face. From the point where the magistral of the cut intersects the tangent, set off 11.0 yards, which is the width of the cut on the interior. This point joined with the point on the exterior, gives the counterscarp of the cut.

A parapet 20 feet thick is made behind the scarp of the cut. The relief of this parapet is so determined that, at the highest point of the magistral, which is the point on the interior, there shall be no exterior slope; which places the interior crest 3.33 feet above the magistral at this point. The scarp wall itself, at this point, is 13 feet above the bottom of the cut on the interior; and the interior line of the bottom is 13 feet nearly, above the bottom of the ditch of the redoubt. These conditions fix the reference of this point of the magistral at (76.17). The interior crest, which is horizontal, is therefore at the reference (79.50).

The bottom of the cut has a slope of 4.80 feet from the interior to the demi-lune scarp; and the magistral of the cut is parallel to the bottom, and at 13 feet above it. This gives the reference of the exterior point of the magistral (71.37). The magistral of the demi-lune, from this exterior point to the point, b, is held horizontal and at the same reference (71.37). The parapet of this portion of the demi-lune face is 12 feet thick; its interior crest is determined, by passing a plane through the interior crest of the parapet behind the cut, and allowing the prolongation of this plane to pass 3 feet above the demi-lune salient. The preceding data are sufficient to determine the lines in question.

**124. Analysis of the Cut.** The cut isolates the part of the demi-lune, near the extremity of the face, from the salient portion; this part being arranged with a parapet behind the cut, can be defended after the enemy has effected a lodgment on the demi-lune salient. The cut thus prevents the enemy from driving the besieged from the redoubt of the reëntering place-of-arms; which he might do, were the whole demi-lune to fall at once into his possession.

The position of the cut is so determined as to allow the face of the demi-lune redoubt to flank the face c′ d′. Widening the cut on the interior facilitates this object.

By making the interior line of the bottom of the cut 13 feet above the bottom of the ditch, the scarp of the demi-lune redoubt is partly covered; and at the same time an obstacle is placed in the way of an enemy, who might attempt to carry the work behind the cut, by first getting into the cut.

It will be seen in examining the demi-lune ditch, that the slope 4.80 feet given to the bottom of the cut, still leaves a height of 15 to 18 feet between the exterior line and the bottom of the demi-lune ditch, which will secure the cut from an assault on that side. The object of this slope is chiefly so to diminish the height of that part of the demi-lune scarp, from the cut to the point, b, that it may not be exposed to a battery, which can be placed on the glacis of the reëntering place-of-arms.

As to the interior crest, it is placed as low as possible; and is arranged to cover the interior from the plunging fire of the enemy when established on the demi-lune salient.

**125. Demi-lune.** (Pl. IV., Fig. 2.) To return to the demi-lune, of which only the magistral and the relief of the interior crest at the salient have been determined. The magistral at the salient is placed 11.40 feet below the interior crest; and as the reference of the latter is (78.0), the reference of the former will be (66.60). The magistral has a slope of 1.50 feet from the salient to the cut; and the interior crest is parallel to the magistral; this condition will determine the interior crest when the salient is known; and this is arranged so as to have a pan-coupé of 4.30 yards.

The scarp wall of the demi-lune is 22.50 feet high.

The terre-plein is 11.0 yards wide. A ramp 3.30 yards

wide, having a slope of $\frac{1}{6}$, leads from the ditch of the demi-lune redoubt to the demi-lune terre-plein. The position and arrangement of the ramp are shown in (Pl. IV., Fig. 2.)

The terre-plein is finished by a slope of earth, instead of being sustained by a wall. The slope is thus arranged: the part terminating the ramp, is a plane of $\frac{1}{1}$; the portion in the angle is formed by an inclined cylindrical surface, which touches the two interior lines of the terre-plein; the width of the ditch at the salient of the redoubt, terminated by the base of the cylinder, is 4.30 yards. The remaining portion of the slope is formed of a warped surface, the elements of which are horizontal, connecting the cylinder and the plane of $\frac{1}{1}$. This construction is purely arbitrary; the object being to have the portion of the slope in the salient as gentle as practicable, so that this part may serve as a ramp for infantry.

**126. Analysis of the Demi-lune, etc.** The principal properties of the demi-lune were mentioned in describing Cormontaingne's method; and it was there observed that he improved upon Vauban's, by augmenting the dimensions of the demi-lune. Engineers, since Cormontaingne, finding that the demi-lune still admitted of being enlarged with advantage, have accordingly so determined its dimensions, that it may be thrown so far to the front as will still place the breach, which an enemy may make in its face, within the range of the musketry of the bastion-face. In large fronts, like this under consideration, the demi-lune may be thus made to cover about 30 yards of the bastion-faces from the shoulder angle; and thus secure retrenchments resting against this part, from being turned by a breach made near the shoulder angle.

These considerations limit the salient angle of the demi-lune to 60°; and place the salient at not more than 210 yards from the bastion-face, as this distance will bring the breach at about 180 yards from this face, or within the effective range of musketry.

The demi-lune thus arranged, places the bastions, in all cases, in strong reënterings; but when the angles of the polygon are very obtuse, the faces of the bastions prolonged also fall within the salients of the demi-lunes, and are, therefore, not easily enfiladed.

The fire from the demi-lune is very effective on the enemy's works along the bastion capitals. Finally, it is a work of which the enemy can only obtain possession after great labor and loss of time; and when carried, it is with great difficulty that he can render it tenable, as it is exposed to the fire of the enceinte, within a short range.

The demi-lune, with these advantages, is not without defects. Its faces, from their position, are exposed to an enfilading fire; it deprives the curtain of all action on the exterior ground; and it is only when the angles of the bastion are very open that the reënterings formed by the demi-lunes become of a formidable character. The glacis of the demi-lune covered-way forms a ridge, which is serviceable to the enemy by masking his works on one side of the ridge from the fire of the collàteral works on the other.

Having noticed these general properties of the demi-lune, the further particular constructions may be examined.

In terminating the face at 11.0 yards from the exterior side, a passage made along the extremity of this face, and a face-cover for the bastion, of which mention will be made further on, are allowed for; moreover, the flank of the demi-lune redoubt, intended to defend the breach in the bastion-face by a reverse fire, is unmasked by it.

The command of the curtain over the demi-lune is reduced to the minimum; and to obtain as much interior space for the demi-lune redoubt as practicable, the height of the interior crest above the magistral is fixed at 11.40 feet, the interior space evidently depending on this height. The terre-plein is reduced to 11.0 yards, partly for the same reason, and partly to give an enemy great trouble in establishing a battery on it, as to do this he will be obliged to cut away a part of the parapet, and will thus expose the rear of the battery to the fire from collateral works.

The terre-plein is terminated by a slope of earth, for economy, and also because this slope is favorable to offensive movements, made to drive the enemy from the breach.

It is not probable that an enemy would attempt to carry the demi-lune by escalade; it is well, however, to provide against such an attempt, in so important a work; it is chiefly on this account that the scarp wall is made 22.50 feet high. This dimension also allows the bottom of the cut to be so placed that it can be swept by the fire of the demi-lune redoubt.

**127.** From the exposed position of the demi-lune terre-plein to enfilading fire, in the methods of Vauban, Cormontaingne, and Noizet, various devices have been proposed by engineers to remedy this defect.

Some have proposed raising a very high bonnet at the salient, to act as a traverse and limit the effect of a plunging enfilade. Others have proposed a curved pan-coupé in the salient, of sufficient size to mount several guns to fire in the direction of the capital. Others suggest breaking the faces into several crotchets, like the covered-way, and with like purpose. Others propose to draw the salient of the parapet so far inwards that the faces prolonged will fall without the limits of the assailant's enfilading positions. Others propose to occupy the salient with a high casemated traverse, to cover from enfilade, and to give a strong fire from the casemates on the assailant's approaches in advance of the salients of the adjacent works.

**128. Face-cover of the Bastion.** (Pl. III., Fig. 3, and Pl. IV., Fig. 1.) By prolonging the bastion counterscarp to the point, f′, it serves as a face-cover to the bastion scarp, masking it from the fire of the breach battery erected around the salient place-of-arms of the demi-lune covered-way. The angle f″ of the face-cover is placed on the same line as the extremity of the double caponnière, for the purpose of covering the troops as they débouche from the caponnière, from the enemy's establishment along the glacis of the bastion covered-way. The height of the wall at the point, f″, is so determined as to intercept the enemy's fire, coming from a point 3 feet above the crest of the bastion covered-way, and passing at 7.50 feet above the bottom of the ditch, at the extremity of the caponnière. From the point f″ to the gorge of the redoubt of the reëntering place-of-arms, the top of the wall ascends, so as to cover the ramp leading from the ditch to the top of the counterscarp at f f′; and also the passage leading from this point to the gorge of the redoubt.

**129. Single Caponnière, and Traverse in the Demi-lune Ditch.** This last passage is also covered from the enemy's works on the glacis of the demi-lune salient place-of-arms, by the crest of a single caponnière, in the ditch of the demi-lune. The glacis of this work is determined by passing a plane through the point (83.40) of the interior crest of the bastion-face, found by producing back the demi-lune magistral, and through two other points in the demi-lune ditch; one taken at 13 feet below the ditch of the redoubt of the reëntering place-of-arms, the other at about 16.50 feet below the cut in the demi-lune. The crest of the caponnière is held in this plane; and in projection is drawn parallel to the magistral of the face-cover, so as to allow space enough between it and the foot of the wall, which terminates the demi-lune face, for a banquette tread of 2 yards, and its slope of $\frac{1}{1}$; all of which will require about 4.30 yards. The passage referred to is 4.30 yards wide. In order that it shall be covered by the crest of the caponnière, the bottom of it must be at least 8 feet below the crest.

The preceding construction subserves two purposes. 1st. From the position of the glacis, it is swept by the fire of the bastion-face; so that the dead space, which was noticed at this point of the demi-lune ditch in Cormontaingne's method, is here removed.

2d. It covers the troops crossing the demi-lune ditch from the fire coming from the demi-lune salient place-of-arms.

As it is important to keep this passage open, even after the enemy obtains possession of the demi-lune, a traverse is placed at the extremity of the caponnière, so as to cover the postern which communicates with the terre-plein of the redoubt of the reëntering place-of-arms. A portion of this traverse has to be sustained by a wall, which is so arranged as to afford the least possible shelter to an enemy, who, from behind it, might attempt to carry the redoubt by the gorge.

The face-cover is terraced, the embankment being 2.50 yards thick at top, and sloped inwards towards the passage.

The details of this part of the construction, being rather complicated, will be better understood by referring to Pl. IV., Fig. 1, than by any written explanation.

**130. Mask in the Demi-lune Redoubt Ditch.** (Pl. IV., Fig. 1). To cover the curtain wall from a fire through the opening between the flank and the tenaille, coming from a battery established on the demi-lune terre-plein, an embankment is formed in the ditch of the demi-lune redoubt; the wall, which separates this ditch from that of the enceinte, being built high enough to support the embankment.

The embankment is sloped on top and terminates in a point near the demi-lune cut; being terminated on the side towards the redoubt, by a slope, the foot of which is 4.30 yards from the foot of the redoubt scarp. The crest of the embankment is on the line drawn through the shoulder angle of the redoubt and the angle of the tenaille.

The bottom of the ditch, between the embankment and redoubt, is about 12 feet above that of the enceinte ditch, which secures the demi-lune from being turned through this ditch.

By separating the embankment from the demi-lune redoubt, this work is secured from any attempt to carry it from the embankment. For the same reason, the gorge wall behind the cut is raised 13 feet above the top of the embankment. A like expedient is resorted to in all similar cases; as in the gorge wall of the redoubt of the reëntering place-of-arms, and the counterscarp of the demi-lune cut, as shown in the details on Pl. IV., Fig.1.

**131. Covered-ways.** (Pl. V., Figs. 1, 2.) The bastioned covered-way is 11.0 yards wide; the interior crest being drawn parallel to the counterscarp.

The crests of the reëntering place-of-arms are drawn parallel to the magistral of the redoubt, and 20 yards from it.

The crest of the demi-lune covered-way is a broken crémaillère, or crotchet line. The short branches of the crémaillère are 6.60 yards long, and are perpendicular to the direction of the demi-lune capital.

**132. Remarks on the Traverses and the Defiles.** The objects of the short branches of the crotchets are to cover the defiles, or passages, between the ends of the traverses and the crest of the covered-way; and to give a column of fire in the direction of the demi-lune capital. To fulfil this last object, the short branches are provided with a banquette, with a slope of only $\frac{1}{1}$, to bring the crest of this branch as near as practicable to the traverse. A passage of 2.0 yards is left between the foot of the banquette slope and the wall, which terminates the end of the traverse; the direction of this wall is parallel both to the long and short branches of the crotchets; leaving a passage between it and the long branch 2.0 yards wide.

To find the position of the short branch, the base of the interior slope being 1.5 feet; the banquette tread 6 feet; the base of the banquette slope 3.50 feet, and the width of the defile 6 feet: 17 feet, or 5.66 yards, is the entire distance sought between the crest of the short branch and the wall that terminates the traverse, parallel to this branch.

The portion of the long branch, opposite the traverse, is without a banquette, &c., for the purpose of leaving the least distance between the crest of the crotchet and the traverse; so that the defile may be covered in the best manner. To effect this, a vertical wall is placed parallel to the end of the traverse, and at 2.0 yards from it, to leave space for the defile; this wall sustains the earth, but is not built up higher than within 1.50 feet of the crest. The earth of the glacis has the natural slope of $\frac{1}{1}$, from the crest to the top of the wall; the base of this slope, consequently, will be 1.50 feet, and a berm of 0.50 feet being left on the top of the wall. These distances added together give 2.66 yards for the distance between the crest of the long branch and the wall parallel to it, which terminates the traverse.

**133. Traverses on the Demi-lune Covered-way.** There are four traverses on the demi-lune covered-way; which, to avoid repetitions, will be designated as No. 1, No. 2, No. 3, and No. 4; No. 1 being nearest the reëntering place-of-arms.

To construct the crotchets of traverses Nos. 1 and 2, a line, l m, is drawn parallel to, and at 13.0 yards from the demi-lune counterscarp; parallel to this line, and at a distance of 6.60 yards, measured on a perpendicular to the demi-lune capital, a second line, l′ m′, is drawn. The salient and reëntering angles of the crotchets, between Nos. 1 and 2, rest on these two lines.

To construct traverse No 1, a line, n n′, is drawn, parallel to l′m′, and at 2.66 yds.; from the point of intersection, n, of this line with the crest of the reëntering place-of-arms, a line, n o, is drawn, so that its intersection, o, with the demi-lune counterscarp, shall be perpendicular to a line drawn from o, to the point a, on the demi-lune. The line, n o, is the interior crest of No. 1. The exterior crest, n′o′, is parallel to it, and at 6.66 yards.

From the point n′ as a centre, with a radius of 5.66 yds., an arc is described; a tangent drawn to this arc, perpendicular to the demi-lune capital, gives the short branch of the crochet.

To construct traverse No. 2: from the extremity of the short crochet, just found, with a radius of 6.60 yds., an arc is described; a tangent drawn from the point, a, to this arc, will give, by its intersection, o, with the counterscarp, a point of the interior crest of No. 2; the interior crest is drawn from this point, perpendicular to the tangent. The exterior crest, n′o′, is drawn at 4.33 yds. from n o.

To obtain the crochets, from any assumed point, n′, of this exterior crest, with radii of 2.66 and 5.66 yds., two arcs are described; tangents are drawn to these arcs; one from the inner extremity of the short branch of No. 1, to the arc of 2.66 yds.; the other to the arc of 5.66 yds. and perpendicular to the demi-lune capital. If these two tangents intersect on the line l′m′, then the point n′ is one point of the end No. 2; and the line n n′ is drawn parallel to the long branch. If the tangents do not intersect on l′m′, then some other point, n′, must be chosen, and a similar construction made, until the intersection is found on the line l′m′, which will be the salient angle of the crotchets.

To construct No 3 and its crotchets, a point is taken on the short branch of the crotchet last found, at 4.30 yds. from its salient angle; from this point an arc is described, with a radius of 4.50 yds.; a tangent drawn to this arc from the point, a, will give the point, o, on the counterscarp, where the interior crest of No. 3 is to be drawn, perpendicular to the tangent. The exterior crest of this traverse is at 4.33 yds. from the interior crest.

The short branches of the crotchets of No. 3 and No. 4, have the same direction as the others; but they are limited by two lines, one drawn parallel to the counterscarp, and at 11.0 yds. from it, the other at 6.60 yds. from this, measured on a perpendicular to the demi-lune capital. These two lines being drawn, the position of the salient and reëntering angles of the crotches that rest upon them, will be found by a construction similar to the one just described.

The reëntering angle of the crotchet of No. 2 is cut off, by drawing a line through the centre of the arc and parallel to the tangent drawn to it from a.

To construct No. 4, commence by finding the foot of its exterior slope; this is done by describing an arc from the angular point, c′, of the redoubt of the reëntering place-of-arms, with a radius of 4.30 yds.; a tangent drawn to this arc, through the demi-lune salient, being produced to the covered-way, gives the foot of the exterior slope. The interior crest of No. 4 is parallel to this line; its position is found, by allowing 4.66 ft., or 1.55 yds., for the base of the exterior slope, and 20 ft., or 6.66 yds., for the thickness of parapet. Having the exterior and interior crests, the point n′ and the crotchets are found as in the preceding cases.

The interior crest of the salient place-of-arms is on the line l m produced; which is at 11.0 yds. from the counterscarp. A pan-coupé of 4.30 yds. is made in the salient.

**134. Traverse on the Bastion Covered-way.** (Pl. V., Fig. 1.) To construct the traverse and its crotches, on the bastion covered-way, a line, t r, is drawn at 5.50 yds., parallel to the crest of the bastion covered-way; the extremity of the traverse, n n′, is drawn parallel to t r, and 2.60 yds. from it. From the point n, on the crest of the reëntering place-of-arms, the interior crest of the traverse is drawn perpendicular to the bastion counterscarp. The exterior crest is 20 ft., or 6.66 yds., from the interior crest.

To find the other branch of the crotchet, nn′ is taken equal to 5.0 yds.; a line is drawn through r and n′, and produced to s, on the crest of the bastioned covered-way; an arc with a radius of 2.66 yds. is now described from n′, and the tangent s t drawn to this arc, is the branch required.

**135. Command of the Covered-way and Traverses.** (Pl. IV., Fig. 2.) To arrange the relief of the covered-way and traverses, the following method is pursued. The salient of the demi-lune covered-way is 7.50 ft. lower than the salient of the demi-lune; the reference of this point then is (70.50.) The interior crests of the salient place-of-arms of traverse No. 4 and the long branch between Nos. 3 and 4 are held in the same plane; the scale of declivity of which is parallel to the demi-lune capital; its inclination being determined by placing the extremity of the long branch, just referred to, 0.75 feet lower than the salient of the demi lune covered-way.

The short branch of the crotchet of No. 3 has the same reference as the salient of the covered-way (70.50). This line, the interior crest of No. 3 and the long branch, are held in the same plane, whose scale of declivity is parallel to the demi-lune capital, and whose inclination is such that, being produced, it will pass 3 feet above the salient of the covered-way.

The relief of No. 2 and its crotchets is determined in the same manner as in the preceding case; the reference of the short branch being fixed at (70.20).

The salients of the bastion covered-way and the reëntering place-of-arms command the salient of the demi-lune covered-way by 1.50 feet. Their reference therefore is (72.0).

**136. Remarks on the Covered-ways and Traverses.** The demi-lune covered-way is made wider towards the reëntering, to cover the traverse defiles with more ease. The width, 11.0 yards, of the portion near the salient, makes the covered-way so narrow, that should an enemy find it necessary to lower his breach battery into it to effect a practicable breach, he will be obliged to cut away a part of the glacis, to obtain sufficient room for his works.

The counterscarp of the redoubt of the reëntering place-of-arms is a slope of earth, so as to make the reëntering place-of-arms more spacious, by joining the ditch to its terre-plein.

The interior crests of the reëntering place-of-arms and its two traverses are held in the same plane; whose scale of declivity is parallel to the bastion capital. This plane produced passes 3 feet above the salients of the salient places of the two collateral demi-lunes, from which this place-of-arms is thus defiled.

The crests of the bastion covered-way are in the same plane; whose scale of declivity is parallel to the bastion capital. This plane, prolonged also, passes 3 feet above the same points as the last mentioned, and for the same object.

The traverses serve as masks to cover the terre-plein of the covered-way from ricochet shots; for this purpose Nos. 2 and 3 may be only 4.33 yards, or 13 feet thick. But the other traverses, which close the reëntering and salient places-of-arms, being more important, have a thickness of 6.66 yards. As the general height of the traverses is 2.66 yards, it is readily seen that, supposing the extreme limit of ricochet firing to be an angle of $\frac{1}{10}$, the traverses should not be more than 26.6 yards apart, in order that a shot striking the crest of one may imbed itself in that immediately in rear of it.

The traverses also serve as a defence; and for this purpose are made like an ordinary parapet. To enable the besieged to defend the covered-way, they are palisaded, and barriers are placed at the defiles. As the means of protracting the defence are only effective when the defiles are perfectly secured from the fire of the enemy, established along the crest of the salient place-of-arms, the reason for the particular construction given for each traverse will now be apparent.

The interior crests of Nos. 1, 2, and 3 are so arranged that they can concentrate their fire on the salient place-of-arms; and each traverse is so combined with the demi-lune as effectually to mask the defile of the one in rear of it.

The defile of No. 1 is masked by No. 2; and a passage of about 2.0 yards at the foot of the banquette slope No. 1 is covered; so that the troops can pass through this defile in perfect safety.

The defile No. 2 is less easily covered by No. 3. To effect it, the inner angle of the crotchet has to be cut off and the banquette slope suppressed, substituting in its place steps; by these means a passage of 1.0 yard is covered, and No. 3 placed not too far from No. 2.

As it is not practicable to cover the defile of No. 3, the position of No. 4 is determined, so as to make the salient place-of-arms as spacious as possible. This is done by placing No. 4 in a position to allow its exterior slope to be swept by the fire of the bastion-face, penetrating between the salient of the demi-lune and the angle of the redoubt of the reëntering place-of-arms.

The defile of the traverse on the bastion covered-way is arranged to prevent any line of fire penetrating through it into the reëntering place-of-arms.

The precautions which are here taken would be still insufficient could the enemy, in possession of the crest of the salient place-of-arms, have a plunging fire upon the covered-way behind the traverses. It is to prevent this that the interior crests of the different traverses, and their respective crotchets, are held in the same plane; which is so arranged that the terre-plein shall be defiled from the enemy's lodgment on the crest of the salient place-of-arms. This arrangement necessarily places the terre-pleins between the traverses on different levels; small ramps will therefore be necessary to pass from one level to another. They are placed at the defiles.

The salient place-of-arms is inclined for the purpose of partially defiling it from the trench cavalier.

Finally, the traverses are sustained on the side of the counterscarp by a profile wall, which is the prolongation of the counterscarp wall; and they are terminated at the other extremity by a wall, so as to make the defile convenient as a communication.

**137. General Remarks.** In the combination and arrangement of the outworks, Noizet has followed closely the methods of Cormontaingne, and of the school of Mézières.

The principal objections to these combinations are:—

1. That from the command given to these works, a considerable portion of the fire of the enceinte, on the site exterior to these works, is obstructed by them. And that some of these works, like the réduit of the demi-lune, and the parapet behind the cut in the demi-lune face, mask the interior of the demi-lune from a portion of this fire.

2. That from the revetted gorges of these works, and the kind of communication between them and the enceinte ditch, sorties on the assailants' works in them, can only be made in small and feeble parties.

3. That the traverses of the covered ways obstruct the free movement of troops along them, and also obstruct the fire of the enceinte on their terre-pleins.

**138.** For these defects various changes have been suggested, and some of them have been adopted in some of the more recent European fortifications.

These consist:—

1. In giving a greater command to the enceinte than that usually found in the methods described.

2. In suppressing the rédnit of the demi-lune, as usually constructed, and replacing it by a casemated réduit placed at the gorge of the demi-lune.

3. In suppressing the traverses of the covered ways except those enclosing the reëntering place-of-arms; depending on the short branches of the crémaillères into which the interior crest of the covered way is broken to limit the effects of enfilade fire.

4. To replace the narrow stairs used by Vauban for communicating with the terre-pleins of the outworks, by wide ramps to facilitate sorties in large bodies.

5. To flank both the covered way and the demi-lune ditch by a casemated réduit placed within the reëntering place-of-arms.

**139.** In every combination the engineer must be guided by the exigencies of the sites that he is called upon to fortify, the character of the defence that it is proposed that the work shall make, and the relative pecuniary cost of different combinations. In taking this last consideration, however, into account, he should not forget that the pecuniary outlay for a work that will protract the defence only a few days longer may often bear no comparison to the benefits arising from it. Had the Malakoff tower at Sebastopol been a stronger work it might have frustrated the last bloody assault of the allies and saved that stronghold of Russia.

**140. Counterscarp of the Bastion and Demi-lune.** Having determined the relief of the covered-way crests, which it may be observed is such that they mask all the masonry of the scarps, and at the same time are so low that an enemy cannot, by the ordinary methods in use, obtain a plunging fire from them upon the terre-pleins of the works in their rear, the position of the counterscarp crests can now be fixed.

The top of the counterscarp wall should be at least 8 feet below the planes of the interior crest of the covered way, and the height of the wall for the body of the place should not exceed 24 feet; and for the demi-lune it may be reduced to 18 feet. These dimensions will therefore be assumed, as the greatest that can be allowed, with a proper regard to economy. And a continuous wall of these heights may be regarded as a powerful auxiliary obstacle, in securing the works from all attempts at surprise.

Adopting the limit of 24 feet for the counterscarp of the bastion, it will be seen that the bottom of the ditch at the foot of this wall is higher than at the foot of the scarp wall of the bastion-face; and as the bottom of the ditch, at the extremity of the double caponnière, has already been determined, these different levels must be connected by planes, combined in the most simple manner.

**141. Cunettes and Bottoms of the Ditches.** (Pls. IV. and V.) A cunette 4.0 yards wide at top, and 3 feet deep, is made in the main ditch to serve as a drain.

A *culvert*, or small arch of masonry, is made under the double caponnière, connecting the cunette on the opposite sides of it. The cunette is placed parallel to the bastion-face; the bottom of the ditch having a slope of 1.50 feet from the foot of the scarp wall to the edge of the cunette, and a slope from the opposite edge up to the foot of the counterscarp wall.

These details will be best understood by referring to (Pls. IV. and V., Fig. 1.) The slopes here given serve to keep the bottom of the ditch dry; they assist in rendering the breach, made in the bastion-face, rather steeper than if the bottom were horizontal; and in the passage of the ditch, the enemy's work is thus more exposed than if the bottom were not sloped from the foot of the counterscarp wall to the cunette.

The demi-lune ditch is arranged upon similar principles. A cunette and culvert are placed in it, to convey the rain-water from it into the main ditch.

**142. Planes of the Glacis.** One principle is chiefly to be attended to in disposing the different planes of the glacis. They should all be swept by the artillery fire of the works immediately in their rear, and by the musketry fire at least of the bastion-face.

The glacis of the bastion covered-way should be swept by the artillery of the bastion-face.

The glacis of the reëntering place-of-arms should be swept by the fire from its réduit.

The glacis of the demi-lune offers more difficulty in its arrangement, owing to the crémaillère form of the interior crests. The best method seems the following:

Planes are passed through each long branch, so as to be swept by the artillery fire of a portion of the face of the demi-lune; these are connected by another series of planes, which are passed through the salient point of each crotchet, and below the plane of musketry fire of at least one-half of the bastion-face, and that of artillery fire of a part of the demi-lune face.

It will be readily seen, from the nature of this problem, that it admits of many solutions. In selecting amongst them, the following considerations may serve as guides:

1. When the planes of the glacis have a very gentle slope, they are better seen by the works in their rear; but the construction is more expensive, on account of the greater quantity of embankment.

2. When the slope is more steep, the enemy's works on the glacis are better exposed to the reverse views of the collateral works, although not so well seen by those directly in rear of the glacis; but the quantity of embankment is smaller.

**143. Outlets, or Sortie Passages.** To communicate from the covered-way with the glacis, an outlet or sortie passage is cut in the least exposed face of the reëntering place-of-arms; and one also on the long branch, between the 3d and 4th traverses.

They are from 3.30 to 4.0 yards wide. The cut is about six feet in depth, the earth being sustained on each side by a profile wall. The bottom of it is a ramp leading from the terre-plein of the covered-way to the top of the glacis. As the outlet is closed by a barrier, it should be arranged at the bottom, to allow the barrier free play in opening and shutting.

**144. Communication of the Enceinte with the Ditch.** The postern of the enceinte leads through the middle of the curtain, descending from the plane of site to the ditch. The inclination of the bottom should never exceed $\frac{1}{6}$. The bottom should not come out upon a level with the bottom of the ditch, but about 6 feet above it; a wooden ramp being used to descend from the postern to the bottom of the ditch.

The width of this postern should be 12 feet; both on account of the greater circulation through it, and because it may be used as a bomb-proof shelter for the troops on duty.

The entrance to this postern, both towards the ditch and the interior, is by door-ways; one through the scarp wall, which closes the postern towards the ditch, and one through a vertical wall of masonry, at the extremity of the enceinte terre-plein, which closes the mouth of the postern towards the interior. The earth of the rampart slope is cut away, to leave the passage to the postern free. The sides of the cut are sustained by wing walls, which make a small angle with the vertical wall of the postern mouth. The door-way may be 7.0 feet wide and 7.50 feet high; the postern itself being 10 feet under the key.

For more security, a partition wall, with a door-way, is sometimes made across the postern, about the middle point. The leaves of the folding-doors here have loop-holes to fire upon an enemy, should he by a surprise gain possession of the exterior door-way.

**145. Communication with the Tenaille.** A postern, for the passage of artillery, is made under the tenaille, and leads to the double caponnière. Two stairs are placed at the gorge of the tenaille, to communicate with its terre-plein.

**146. Communication with the Terre-plein and Ditch of the Demi-lune Rêduit.** Two stairs are placed at the gorge of the demi-lune réduit, to communicate with its terre-plein. A postern for artillery leads from the main ditch to the ditch of the réduit, under its flank, for the communication between the main ditch and the demi-lune.

**147. Communication from the Enceinte Ditch with the Exterior.** To communicate with the covered-ways, a ramp of earth sustained by walls is placed along the wall that terminates the demi-lune and its réduit. This ramp is separated from the extremity of the face-cover by a cut 4.30 yards wide.

**148. Communication with the Demi-lune Cut.** The communication with the work behind the demi-lune cut is by a postern and stair for infantry, which lead from a point on the ramp just described to the terre-plein of the work; passing in a winding direction, under the terre-plein and parapet of the work.

**149. Communications of the Rêduit of the Reëntering Place-of-arms, etc.** The passage behind the single caponnière, in the demi-lune ditch, has already been described. This passage leads to a postern for artillery, made through the face of the réduit, to its ditch. From the ditch a ramp for artillery leads to the terre-plein of the reëntering place-of-arms, and from it to the sortie passage. At the angle of the réduit on the demi-lune ditch, stairs are placed to ascend to its ditch; a ramp for infantry leads from the ditch on this side to the terre-plein.

To ascend to the terre-plein of the réduit, a small postern for infantry is made through the face to the ditch, being placed alongside the postern just described; from this a winding postern and stairs lead to the terre-plein of the réduit.

The foregoing, with what has been said respecting the caponnières, traverse defiles, etc., completes the description of the communications of the front.

**150. Interior Retrenchments.** When a breach is made in the enceinte, although military usage and a point of honor require of the garrison to sustain at least one assault, the consequences of defeat are of too serious a character to expect such an effort, unless a place of safety is provided, into which the garrison may retreat, after defending the breach, and obtain an honorable capitulation. On this account, and also to lengthen the defence, interior retrenchments are made in the bastions.

These works may be either of a temporary or permanent character; but it is generally conceded that the latter class alone offers a serious obstacle to the enemy. The former, moreover, requires that the bastion should be full; and that the retrenchment should be thrown up during the siege, an undertaking of great difficulty, both from the annoyance of the enemy's fire, and the fatigued state of the garrison, occasioned by its ordinary duties.

Therefore, only the permanent interior retrenchments with a revetted scarp and counterscarp will be here given; and which may be regarded as constituent elements of a regularly fortified front.

Noizet, like Cormontaingne, proposes four classes of interior retrenchments.

1st. Those that rest against the faces of the bastions.

2d. Those that rest against the flanks.

3d. Those that rest against the two adjacent curtains.

4th. Those that comprehend several bastions.

**151. First class resting on the Faces.** (Pl. VI., Figs. 1, 2, and A, B, Fig. 3.) The first class may be either the form of a cavalier, shut in by cuts across the bastion-faces; an inverted redan; or finally, if the bastion is very open, a small bastion front.

Of this class, the cavalier has been generally employed. The cavalier receiving a relief so great as to give it a plunging fire upon the enemy's works on the glacis of the bastioned covered-way; whilst the interior of the bastion, in advance of the cavalier ditch and of the cuts or ditches across the bastion terre-plein, between the scarps of the bastion and cavalier, is swept, and the breach that might be made in the bastion salient is defended from the parapets behind the cuts; these parapets, with the portions of the cavalier faces in advance of them, forming the interior retrenchment.

This class presents the advantages of defending the breach within a short distance; and by enclosing the flanks of the bastion within them, they preserve the flanking arrangements of the body of the place until the retrenchment is carried. The principal objection to them is, that by a breach made at the shoulder angle, the enemy can turn them.

**152. Second class resting against the Flanks.** (Pl. VI., Figs. 4 and C.) The second class may be of an inverted redan, or a small bastion front; or finally, of a redan resting against the middle of the flanks, its faces having such a direction that its ditch may be swept by the fire of the flanks of the adjacent bastions.

The last form admits of defending the breach within a short distance; it preserves also the flanking arrangements of the enceinte, and can only be turned by a breach made in the curtain. To sweep its ditch from the opposite flank, it will be necessary to cut down a part of the scarp wall of the flank on which the ditch rests, which will make the height of the wall less than 11.0 yards, and somewhat expose the enceinte to escalade.

**153. Third class resting on two adjacent Curtains.** (Pl. VI., Fig. 4, D.) The third class is usually of the form of a bastioned front. But as the fire of its faces would be masked by the curtain of the enceinte, it is generally best to construct the front simply with a curtain and two flanks.

This class, being thrown farther from the salient of the bastion, does not defend the breach so directly as the two preceding; but its position is stronger, and will force an enemy to employ more means to carry it. From its dimensions, it will require more space on the interior, and will be also more expensive than either of the preceding forms.

**154. Fourth class enclosing several Fronts.** The fourth class, which is placed in the rear of several bastions of the conceinte, or properly several fronts, is a kind of second enciente within the first. An arrangement of this character would of course require a peculiar locality, and would seldom find an application.

**155. Cavalier with cuts in the Bastion Faces.** (Pl. VI., Figs. 1, 2.) The faces of this work are parallel to those of the bastion in which it is placed; its ditch should be about 18 feet below the bastion terre-plein; its scarp wall about 24 feet high. And it may be here observed that all interior retrenchments, to oppose a serious obstacle to an enemy, should have revetments of about these dimensions.

The interior crest of the face should be so high that the line of fire from the salient of the cavalier to the salient of the bastion covered-way shall pass above the bastion salient.

By placing the counterscarp of the cavalier at 14.0 yards

from the interior crest of the bastion, allowing 11.0 yards for the width of the ditch, and making the bottom of the ditch 18 feet below the bastion terre-plein; it will be found that the reference of the bottom of the ditch will be (58.50); the scarp wall being 24 feet high, the reference of its magistral will be (82.50). Now, if the reference of the interior crest be taken at (97.50), or 15 feet above the magistral, its projection will be at 33.16 feet, or 11.06 yards from the magistral; and as both the lines are horizontal, parallel to it. Drawing then three lines parallel to the bastion interior crest, at the distances above mentioned, the projections of the counterscarp, scarp, and interior crest of the cavalier are obtained. The position here given to the interior crest of the face will satisfy the condition first laid down.

The interior crest of the flank is also horizontal; its reference, therefore, is (97.50); the direction of the flank is perpendicular to the line of defence of the bastion; the flank, moreover, is not revetted like the face, but is terminated by prolonging its exterior slope to the bastion terre-plein; the lowest point of the foot of this exterior slope will therefore be about (73.00), the reference of the bastion terre-plein at the extremity of its flank; the least width of the bastion terre-plein, between its flank and that of the cavalier, should be 14.0 yards. If, then, from the interior angle of the curtain, with a radius of 14.0 yards, an arc be described, and a tangent be drawn to this arc, perpendicular to the line of defence, this tangent may be taken as the horizontal of the exterior slope of the cavalier flank, whose reference is (73.0); the interior crest of the flank is drawn parallel to this horizontal, and at 41.16 feet or 13.72 yards from it; which will be the distance found by calculation, the thickness of the parapet being 20 feet, the superior slope $\frac{1}{6}$, and the exterior slope $\frac{1}{1}$.

The length of the flank is found by drawing through the angle of the curtain a line parallel to the line of defence, and where it cuts the interior crest of the flank will be the extremity of the flank.

To terminate the gorge of the cavalier, a plane of $\frac{1}{1}$ is passed through the extreme points of the interior crest of its flanks. A passage of 4.30 yards is left on the bastion terre-plein, at the gorge of the cavalier, to communicate with it, and also to preserve an uninterrupted communication between the two adjacent curtains. A ramp 3.30 yards wide, with a slope of $\frac{1}{6}$, leads from the gorge of the cavalier to its terre-plein. This ramp is generally placed along the capital of the bastion.

**156. Cuts in the Bastion Faces.** (Pl. VI., Figs. 1, 2.) To determine the cut across the bastion-face, a distance of 13.0 yards is a set-off from the shoulder angle of the bastion, along its interior crest; from this point a line is drawn, making an angle of 100° with the interior crest; this line being produced to intersect the magistral of the cavalier face, is the interior crest of the parapet behind the cut. The reference of this line where it intersects the magistral is (82.50), the reference of the other extremity being (84.0): it is held in the same plane with the portion of the interior crest of the bastion, between the shoulder angle and the point at 13.0 yards from it; the reference of the shoulder angle remaining as already found; it will be seen that the plane of these two lines produced, passes 3 feet above the bastion salient. The thickness of a parapet is only 12 feet.

The magistral of the scarp of the cut is horizontal, its reference being (76.50). From the preceding data, its position is easily determined. A line drawn parallel to the magistral, and at 6.60 yards from it, will be the counterscarp of the cut. The counterscarp wall of the cut is carried up to the top of the bastion face, and forms a profile wall to sustain the earth. The scarp wall of the cut is of the same height as that of the cavalier; the bottom of the cut will therefore be referenced (52.50); a portion of the ditch of the cavalier face has the same reference; this portion is found by holding at the level (58.50), that part of the bottom of the ditch towards the salient which can be swept by the fire of the parapet behind the cut; placing the bottom of the remaining portion, towards the cut, on the same level as the bastion of the cut, or at the reference (52.50); the two levels being separated by a vertical wall 6 feet high which retains the earth of the upper level.

**158.** This arrangement of the ditch of the cavalier subjects only a part of it to the fire of the parapet behind the cut. By placing the door of the postern that leads into the cavalier ditch, at the point where the vertical wall separates the two levels, it will be partially covered from the enemy's lodgment on the bastion terre-plein.

**159.** The object of the cut is similar to the one in the demi-lune face; it confines the enemy to the salient part of the bastion, preventing him from extending his works along the bastion terre-plein, to turn the cavalier by its gorge; so that to obtain possession of this work, he must make a breach in its face.

**160.** There is a dead space in the cavalier ditch, throughout the lower level, which might offer some advantages were the enemy to attempt to carry the parapet of the cut by escalade. To remedy this defect, it has been proposed to place a crenated gallery behind the scarp wall of the cut, to flank the entire ditch.

**161.** The disposition of the cavalier and cuts within the bastion does not leave sufficient space upon the terre-plein of the latter to organize a covered-way. But in the retrenchments of open bastions, resting on the flanks or curtains, to which the form of a tenaille or small bastioned front is given, a covered-way, with a reëntering place-of-arms closed by traverses, can be organized, which will give considerable additional confidence and security in the defence of the breach in the bastion with the bayonet; as this coverėd-way will cover the retreat of the troops guarding the breach into the ditch of the retrenchment; whereas, when the counterscarp is not secured in this manner, the retreating body run the risk either of being cut off or of having the enemy follow so closely on their heels as to force their way into the retrenchment, and deprive the defence of this last resort for making favorable terms of surrender.

The organization of these covered-ways presents no peculiarity. They should, as far as practicable, be defiled from the besieger's lodgments within the bastion assailed.

## VI.

### CHOUMARA'S METHOD.

**162.** Choumara, a French officer of engineers of distinguished abilities, is the author of several remarkable memoirs on the defects of the bastion system, and the means by which they may be removed and very additional strength be thereby given to the defences. His propositions for this purpose may be briefly stated as follows:

1. That part of a permanent work which can undergo no modification during the progress of a siege is the masonry, and it may therefore be regarded as the really permanent feature; all the parts of earth, as the parapets, &c., being susceptible of such modifications as circumstances may demand.

This Choumara terms *the independence of the parapets as respects the scarps.*

The latter, upon which the security of the work against an open assault or a surprise depends, must necessarily receive a direction, such that it can be swept by the flanking arrangements, a necessity that does not exist for the parapets, which may receive any direction compatible with the interior space.

The parapets may therefore be thrown back from the salients, as in the bastion (Pl. XIX., Fig. 1), and receive a curvilinear form to throw a greater volume of fire in the direction of the capital.

Or they can be retired from the faces, as in the bastion (Fig. A), for the purpose of giving them such directions that their prolongations shall cut the adjacent demi-lunes, and thus be masked from enfilading views.

Or they may be prolonged so as to afford a greater column of flank fire, as in the flanks 1, (Fig. 1,) or they may be broken into any direction for the same purpose, or to give a more effective direction to their fire.

Or, finally, they may be thrown back from the scarp walls instead of resting immediately upon them, and thus render a breach less practicable, since the whole, or a portion of the parapet, will still retain its place after the breach has been made in the scarp, depending on the distance at which the parapet has been moved back.

In all of these cases of the application of the independence of the parapets, Choumara proposes to convert the space left between the foot of the parapet and the scarp wall into a *chemin de ronde*, or corridor, which is covered in front by a slight parapet, and from enfilading fire by giving an increased height to the portion of the parapet adjacent to the salients, forming a *bonnet*, as in Figs. 1, A, B, &c. This corridor is occupied by sharpshooters to annoy the besieger's trenches. Furthermore, Choumara regards the corridor as an additional security against surprise and escalade.

2. Choumara proposes to place high traverses in the bastion salients, to cover the faces from enfilade and the flanks from reverse views, and similar traverses at the shoulder angles with the same object. These he also proposes to casemate, or else construct with blindages for artillery to obtain a fire in the directions of the capitals, and reverse views on the demi-lune glacis and the breach in the bastion face. As these traverses, from their height, might give the besiegers in possession of them a plunging fire on the bastion retrenchments, he proposes so to arrange them that they can

be readily destroyed at any moment by mines, or, if of timber, be burned.

3. To mask the masonry of the enceinte and demi-lune from breaching batteries, erected in their usual positions along the crests of the glacis, Choumara proposes to form what he terms an *interior glacis*, or covering mass of earth, in the ditches, the crests of which shall mask the masonry of the scarps from the positions in question; and the upper surface of which, forming a glacis, shall be swept by the fire of the works in its rear. In this manner he expects to force the besiegers to the difficult operation of making lodgments in this glacis to obtain suitable positions for their breaching batteries.

4. By selecting for some of his outworks those points on the exterior which are most favorable to the action of the assailant's sharpshooters, he proposes in this way to cripple this important means of attack.

5. By giving greater extent to the exterior side, and a more retired position to the curtain, which is also to be made as short as possible, Choumara obtains bastions of ample size, not only to admit of the modifications he proposes for the parapets, traverses, and *chemins de ronde*, but for strong interior retrenchments, so organized with bomb-proof shelters, and arranged defensively towards the interior, that each bastion will admit of a defence to the rear at its gorge, after the besiegers may have effected a breach at other points and penetrated within the enceinte.

**163. Plan.** In adapting these propositions for a bastioned front, Choumara proposes, in order to obtain the requisite room in the interior of the bastions and a large increase of flank fire, to take the exterior side from 400 to 600 metres, French. In the front (Fig. 1, Pl. XIX), for example, the exterior side is 440 metres; the lines of defence are drawn through a point on the perpendicular of the front at 74 metres, or one-sixth of 440 metres within the exterior side; the faces are 150 metres, and the flanks, drawn perpendicular to the lines of defence, are 85 metres, a length which prolongs them 35 metres within their intersections with the lines of defence.

By this construction the curtain, which will be 115 metres long, will be well swept, and the gun at the curtain angle can be brought to bear on the one of the besieger's counter-battery against the flanks which are furthest out, thus giving a very great preponderance in fire to the flank over the counter battery.

The deep reëntering thus formed between the flanks and curtains gives ample room for a tenaille with flanks for four guns; these guns are covered in flank by a traverse. The tenaille is not revetted in front of its curtain and flanks, or at its gorge. It masks sufficiently the scarp of the flanks, and curtain of the enceinte, to prevent any danger to the latter from the destruction of the portion of the scarp wall that can be seen over the tenaille.

**164.** The salient of the demi-lune is the vertex of an equilateral triangle, the base of which is drawn between two points on the bastion faces, at 18 metres from the shoulder angles. The faces of the demi-lune, D, are 144 metres, and revetted. The parapet of the demi-lune is thrown back from the revetment, leaving a corridor covered by a parapet at the foot of its exterior slope. The parapet is broken near the gorge, so as to give two short flanks of 13 metres perpendicular to the exterior side. The salient is occupied by a casemated traverse with flanks for three guns. This traverse masks the interior of the demi-lune and the corridor from enfilading views. A disposition is shown for cuts across the demi-lune faces, the parapets of which are to be thrown up after the siege commences. The demi-lune ditch is 17 metres wide. The portion of this ditch towards the gorge slopes upward as a glacis, and is swept by the fire of the enceinte.

**165.** The interior glacis of the demi-lune commences at the counterscarp of this work and has a glacis slope outwards, its width being 45 metres. Here commences the revetted gorge of the covered-way. The width of the covered-way is 10 metres. Its interior crest is an indented line. There are no traverses in this work unless required for its defilement.

**166.** A spacious and strong réduit is placed in the demi-lune salient place-of-arms. Its faces are 132 metres long, and revetted. Its parapet is thrown back, leaving a corridor in front of it, and is curved at the salient for five guns, sweeping along the capital. A bonnet is placed in its salient to cover the corridor from enfilade, and two traverses for the same object on its terre-plein. This réduit forms a mask for the portion of the demi-lune occupied by the traverse.

**167.** Choumara places strong réduits, M, with revetted scarps and gorges in the reëntering place-of-arms. The parapets of these works are curved at the salients for batteries to sweep the approaches on the bastion capitals and the demi-lune glacis, and they are thrown back from the scarp walls to give a corridor for sharpshooters. As these réduits are necessarily contracted, Choumara prefers to them a strong réduit of larger dimensions, placed in the bastion salient place-of-arms and organized like the preceding.

**168.** One of the most striking features of Choumara's modifications is the mode in which he proposes to organize the large bastions, with defences which shall serve as an interior retrenchment, in case the bastion is one of the points of attack; or convert the bastion into an isolated fort or citadel for the garrison, in case the besieger gains possession of the interior of the enceinte through an assault at some other point. This he proposes to accomplish by increasing the lengths of the exterior side, and also of the bastion flanks.

**169.** With this object Choumara places a row of casemates within the bastions, on a line perpendicular to their capitals. Each casemate is from 60 to 80 feet long, from 12 to 20 feet wide, and 12 feet high. This row of casemates serves as a curtain both for the retrenchment of the bastion and for the defence of the gorge against an interior attack. For the defence of the salient portion of the bastion a cut is made across each face and extended to the capital. The scarp of this cut is made into the form of a bastion front with orillons at the shoulder angles; the casemates forming the curtain of this front. The counterscarp of the cut may be either revetted, or have a simple slope of earth. In the latter case the bottom of the ditch of the front at the foot of the scarp wall is at a suitable level to admit of an efficient height of scarp wall to secure it from escalade. A broad ramp leads from the centre casemate, along the capital, towards the bastion salient, to the counterscarp of the cut, and there branches into two other ramps leading up to the bastion terre-plein on the right and left. Until the besiegers are about to breach the bastion-faces their parapets are left intact; and the portions of the cut along which the parapets run are filled up, as in the bastion on the right, thus leaving a free communication throughout the interior of the bastion. So soon as it is thought necessary to cut off this communication and to get the retrenched portion in a state of defence, that part of the parapet across the cuts is demolished; the cut excavated and suitably arranged; and the parapet of the retrenchment formed in part of the earth arising from these changes. The parapet of the front of the retrenchment is thrown back, leaving a corridor for sharpshooters covered by a slight parapet; that portion of this corridor along the retired flank being covered by the earthen mask of the orillon. Choumara further proposes, where there is a probability of the scarp of the bastion-face, which closes the cut on the exterior, being opened, so that a breach might be made by firing through it on the flank of the retrenchment, to run the scarp wall of the retrenchment at right angles across the cut, as shown on the right face of the left bastion, and to arrange the bastionnet, which this modification would give at the shoulder angle, for sharpshooters.

**170.** To expose the interior of the retrenchment to the fire of the flanks of the adjacent bastions, and to the parapet of a second retired interior retrenchment resting on the two curtains adjacent to the bastion of attack, a portion of the parapet of the bastion flanks, near the curtain, is demolished, and a slope is given to the portion of the terre-plein on which it rested. The retired interior retrenchment Choumara proposes to make of earth in the form of a bastioned front, breaking the faces in the most suitable manner to sweep the rear of the retrenchment in its front.

**171.** The dispositions for converting the bastion into a citadel are similar to the preceding, consisting of a small front, the faces of which are nearly in the prolongations of the adjacent curtains, with orillons to cover the corridor of the retired flank. This front has a covered-way and glacis in advance of it, the crest of which masks the scarp.

**172.** Choumara has made an ample provision for easy communications between all points of the enceinte and the outworks, so placing them as to be well covered from the besieger's fire and well swept by that of the garrison; preferring wide ramps for this purpose. The communication from the enceinte with the main ditch is through gateways in the scarp wall of the curtain, at its extremities. The rampart at these points is removed to the level of the main ditch: the portion of it between them, along the centre of the curtain, being sustained at the ends by revetment walls run back perpendicularly to the scarp wall of the curtain. Ramps lead from the gorges of the bastions down to these outlets into the main ditch. From these outlets the communications to the outworks are around the flanks of the tenaille, and through the enceinte ditch, to ramps placed along the enceinte counterscarp leading into the demi-lune, the demi-lune ditch, the enceinte covered-way, and its redoubts in the places-of-arms; and from the demi-lune ditch to the redoubt of the demi-lune salient place-of-arms. Posterns on the faces and flanks of the bastions, near the shoulder angles, lead to the corridors of the enceinte. Passages are left at the ends of the faces of the outworks leading from their corridors to the interior of the works. To keep open the communication between the bastions, a gallery between their gorges is made along the curtain wall.

For the security of the casemates, barricades can be made in their doors and windows, by means of timber let in grooves made in the walls; the space between the exterior and interior timber facing being filled with sand-bags.

**173. Remarks.** The memoirs in which Choumara brought his propositions before the public naturally attracted attention, as much, perhaps, from their polemical character and piquancy of style as their professional interest. They contain but few things the germs of which are not to be found in writers who preceded him.

His modifications respecting the parapets, throwing them back from the scarps and breaking them into directions best suited for defence, are to be met with in *Chasseloupe's* propositions.

His proposals for lengthening the bastion flanks and occupying the salient places-of-arms by redoubts with considerable command, are to be found in the method of *de la Chiche.*

To *Virgin* he seems to be indebted for his organization of interior retrenchments, which are to convert each bastion into an independent work, equally provided for defence against approaches both from the interior and exterior of the enceinte.

Like disputants, usually, of an ardent temperament, he over-estimates the value of many of his propositions and loses sight of their countervailing defects. By laying down as a principle what may be exceptionally good in practice, he has rather weakened his own positions. This is the case, particularly, with his rule of independence of the parapets on the scarps, which, if adopted in all cases, might demand a greatly increased and hurtful command, and cut up to great disadvantage the interior spaces of the bastions.

His introduction of the *chemins de ronde* on the faces of the bastion and the demi-lune adds really very little, if at all, to the exterior defence; whilst they contract the interior space of these works, break in upon the unity of the defence, and place the troops in them in a very exposed position to the means of annoyance possessed by the besieger.

His expectations with respect to the effect of his fire in the direction of the capitals, in delaying the besieger's approach to the 3d parallel, were hardly warranted by the experience gained in artillery and small-arms, even at the time the last edition of his memoirs appeared. It is hardly to be questioned, now that these weapons have been so greatly improved, both in range and accuracy of fire, that, considering the increased development of the besieger's parallels, which gives him a choice of positions for his batteries on so extended a line, the concentrated fire he could bring to bear on the batteries in question would not only soon ruin their casemates, but would greatly damage the adjacent faces and also the flanks of the bastions, although covered from enfilading views, either by the direction of the parapets of the faces, or the high traverses raised with the same object.

These advantages in the position of the besieger, it is thought, would prevent any delay in pushing forward his approaches up to the 3d parallel. After this the approaches would probably be retarded beyond the usual time in the attack on Cormontaingne's front, owing chiefly to the réduits in the bastion and demi-lune salient places-of-arms, and the arrangement of the face-cover in the enceinte ditch.

**174**. Supposing an enceinte organized according to his method, and containing interior retrenchments to oppose the besieger's approaches both from without and within the enceinte, Choumara estimates at least six separate epochs of breaching batteries, as follows:

1st, against the réduit of the demi-lune salient place-of-arms.

2d, against the demi-lune and the réduit of the bastion salient places-of-arms.

3d, against the bastions.

4th, against the bastion retrenchment; 5th, against the retired retrenchment.

6th, and finally, against the bastions converted into citadels by the fronts with which their gorges are closed.

According to the estimate of the time made by Choumara, it would require 112 days from the opening of the trenches to the final assault and reduction of the last defences.

# CHAPTER III.

## TENAILLED SYSTEM.

### SUMMARY.

Description and analysis of the system (Art. 175).

**175.** Several engineers of professional eminence have proposed tenailled enceintes, as offering defensive properties superior to bastioned enceintes. This system has found but few advocates, and, except in particular localities, where the natural features of the site demanded it, and for small works, it has met with no practical applications.

Requiring that the salient angles shall not be less than 60°, and the reëntering angles between 90° and 100°, the tenailled system is only adapted to regular polygons of a sufficient number of sides to admit of these conditions being satisfied.

If the exterior sides are kept within the limits usually admitted by engineers for bastioned enceintes, the faces of the tenailles become very long, and the reënterings very deep; thus presenting two serious defects, long lines which are very much exposed to enfilade, and a great diminution of the interior space, as compared with the bastioned enceinte.

The ditches when dry can only be swept by casemated defences in the re-entering angles; and even then but partially, unless the casemated embrasures are placed very near the level of the bottom of the ditch, in which case the enceinte would be exposed to a surprise through the embrasures; and, in the contrary case, liable to a like attempt from the dead space at the reënterings below the embrasures. In wet ditches this exposure to surprise would be much less if the ditches could not be forded. In either case the defect arising from embrasure casemates placed in a reëntering angle would be a serious objection to using the guns of each side simultaneously.

When the salient angles of the tenailles are acute, the effect of the enfilading fire would not be felt alone on the face enfiladed, but on the adjacent face or front, and shot passing over would damage the adjacent tenailles.

The foregoing are the chief objections to this system. It presents no advantage but the very illusory one, considering the consequences arising from it, of long faces presenting a mutual flanking and cross fire of considerable extent.

# CHAPTER IV.

## POLYGONAL SYSTEM.

### SUMMARY.

Description and Analysis of the Polygonal System (Art. 176.)—Montalembert's Polygonal Method (Art. 177).

## I.

### POLYGONAL SYSTEM.

**176.** The polygonal system has been proposed by several engineers of distinction, but its most ardent advocate has been the celebrated Montalembert, whose views have been more or less carried out in many of the more recent constructions of Germany.

Consisting of either a simple polygonal enceinte without reënterings, the sides of which are flanked by casemated caponnières, placed at the middle point of the fronts, or of fronts either slightly tenailled or of a bastion form, with short casemated flanks to flank the faces of the central caponnières, this system affords more interior space, and from the mode adopted of flanking the enceinte, will admit of much larger fronts than either the bastioned or the tenailled systems. The salient angles moreover will be more open in this than in the other two systems.

From these peculiarities of this system the positions suitable for the erection of batteries to enfilade the faces of the enceinte are less advantageous, from their being thrown in nearer to the adjacent fronts than in either of the other systems; whilst a greater development of trenches will also be requisite to envelope the fronts of attack.

These obvious advantages, however, are counterbalanced by the want of the concentrated cross-fires which are afforded, in both the bastioned and tenailled systems, in advance of the salients of the enceinte, and upon the ground generally in advance of the fronts.

Each front of the polygonal system offers moreover a long and vulnerable line to enfilading and slant fire, which will also, to some extent, take effect on the reverse of the adjacent fronts.

But the chief objection to this system lies in the mode adopted for flanking the enceinte. The casemated caponnières for this purpose being exterior to the enceinte, it will be exposed to escalade as soon as the fire of the caponnières is silenced, which, considering the structure of the caponnières, and the exposure of their embrasures to the enfilading batteries, will, in all probability, take place at an early period after this fire is opened.

## II.

### MONTALEMBERT'S POLYGONAL METHOD.

**177.** Among the writers on permanent fortification whose works have had an important bearing on the progress of the art, Montalembert holds a conspicuous place, although not educated as an engineer. Struck by the evident defects of the methods of his predecessors, particularly the want of casemates, both for defensive dispositions for artillery and musketry, and the shelter of the garrison and munitions, Montalembert devoted his time, talents, and fortune to bringing about a change in the direction in which it seemed to him called for. His efforts, however, led to no modifications of consequence during his life, which was principally spent in angry controversies with his opponents, except the extension of casemated defences for sea-coast works; and it is only within a comparatively recent period, since the termination of the great wars in Europe, in the present century, that a new school of engineers has grown up in Germany, based upon the views put forth mainly by Montalembert; and that these views have met with favor in other parts, although still opposed by many able engineers in all countries who contest their soundness.

The principal propositions of Montalembert consist: 1. In the entire rejection of the bastioned system, as, according to his views, unsuitable to a good defensive disposition; and in its stead he proposed to use either the *tenailled system*, or else the *polygonal system*.

2. In basing the strength of these last systems upon an overwhelming force of artillery fire in defensive casemates.

3. In organizing strong permanent works within, and independent of the body of the place, which are to serve as a secure retreat for the garrison when forced to give up its defence.

Most of the objections urged against the bastioned system and its outworks having already been adverted to in the analysis of the front, it will be unnecessary to recapitulate them here; and as the tenailled system, composed of faces of equal lengths with reëntering angles of 90°, and salient angles of 60°, and termed by Montalembert *perpendicular fortification*, from the position of the faces at the reënterings, has many obvious and more serious defects than either of the other two, it is proposed to give here a description of the polygonal system alone, and that in its most simple form; the one in which Montalembert presented it for the fortifications at Cherbourg, one of the most important naval stations in France.

**178.** Montalembert first gave the name polygonal system to a traçé of the enceinte in which all of the angles are either salient, or where the reëntering are very slight.

**Plan.** In the traçé proposed for this place, X, Y, (Fig. 1, Pl. XVI.) is the exterior side, or direction of the scarp. The body of the place consists of the scarp wall, D, (Fig. 1,) and section on P Q, arranged with casemates for artillery and musketry; of a corridor, C, between these casemates and the earthen rampart and parapet, B. In rear of the rampart is a high wall, A, arranged with loop-holes, within which the garrison retired when driven from the defence of the rampart.

Casemated caponnières, M, which are secure from a *coup-de-main*, are placed along the rampart, and so arranged that a fire can be thrown from them over the parapet and also along the terre-plein. The corridor, C, is also swept by a casemated caponnière, G, for musketry; and the front of the wall, A, by a like arrangement.

The principal caponnière for flanking the main ditch is in the form of a lunette, and placed at the middle of the exterior side, its flanks joining the casemated gallery, D, of the enceinte. The flanks, H, and the faces, K, of this work, are arranged with two tiers of artillery and musketry fire; each flank carrying ten guns and each face twelve guns. A wet ditch, I, separates the faces and flanks; a loop-holed wall encloses the portion between the flanks, from which the opposite portion between the faces is swept by musketry.

The caponnière is covered in front by a face cover, N, of earth, in the shape of a redan. The scarp of the enceinte is covered in like manner by the continuous face-cover, O, of earth, in the reëntering angles of which casemated batteries of two stories, for artillery and musketry, are placed to flank the ditches and sweep the positions for counter-batteries around the salients of the covered-way. These batteries are masked in front by the earthen works, S and Q. The whole is covered by the glacis of the covered-way, arranged in the usual manner.

The better to flank the main caponnière, the portion of the casemated gallery joining it is arranged with two tiers of artillery fire, the remaining portion having but one tier of guns.

**179. Profiles.** The sections along P Q, R S, and T U, show the relative command of the different works and the width of the ditches and earthen ramparts.

The communications between the different works are by bridges across the wet ditches.

**180.** It is now generally admitted that although Montalembert has rendered important services to the progress of fortification, particularly as regards the more extensive employment of casemated defences, still many of his projects were visionary. How far the recent works constructed in Europe, which are based on his views, will answer their ends, remains to be seen by the test of actual siege operations against them.

The partisans for and against these views are equally confident in their arguments. But with the rapid improvement in artillery which has taken place within the last few years, and the heavier calibre which will doubtless be hereafter used in siege operations, it is very doubtful, from what experience has already shown as to the effects of artillery on casemate defences, whether they will be found to withstand these powerful means, in which case the systems based upon Montalembert's views must fall to the ground.

# CHAPTER V.

## RECENT GERMAN FORTIFICATIONS.

### SUMMARY.



## I.

### RECENT GERMAN FORTIFICATIONS.

**181.** In the large additions made to the fortifications of the German States, since the general peace in Europe in 1815, the German engineers have for the most part of these new structures embraced the ideas put forth in the works of Montalembert and Carnot, adopting for the plan of their enceintes the polygonal system with flanking caponnières, combining with these numerous casemates for defence, for bomb-proof shelters, for quartering the troops and preserving the munitions and other stores.

**182.** From what has been published on this subject by the German engineers themselves and other European writers, the following appear to be the leading features upon which these works are based:

1. To occupy the principal assailable points of the position to be fortified by works which shall contain within themselves all the resources for a vigorous defence by their garrisons; these works being placed in reciprocal defensive relations with each other, but so arranged that the falling of one of them into the besieger's hands will neither compel the loss of the others nor the surrender of the position.

2. To cover the space to the rear of these independent works either by a continuous enceinte, usually of the poly-

gonal system, with a revetted scarp of sufficient height to secure it from escalade; the parts of this enceinte being so combined with the independent works in advance that all the approaches of the besiegers upon each, both during the near and distant defence, shall be swept in the most effective manner by their fire; or else to connect these works by long curtains; or, finally, to employ them, as in a system of detached works, either to occupy important points in advance of the main work, or for forming capacious entrenched camps with a view to the eventualities of a war.

3. To provide the most ample means for an active defence by covered-ways strongly organized with casemated redoubts, and with spacious communications between them and the interior for sorties in large bodies.

4. So to organize the artillery for the near defence that it shall be superior to that of the besiegers at the same epoch, and be placed in positions where it will be sheltered from the besieger's guns up to the time that it is to be brought into play.

**183.** The plan of the independent works may be of any polygonal figure which is best adapted to the part assigned them in the defence of the position; but they are generally in the form of lunettes, (Pl. 23, Fig. 2,) having a revetted scarp and counterscarp to secure them from escalade.

In the gorge of the work a casemated defensive barrack is placed, which serves as a réduit or keep; a simple loop-holed wall which is flanked by the barrack closing the space between it and the flanks of the work, and securing the latter from an assault in the rear. The ditches of the work are either flanked from the enceinte in the rear; or, when the work is a detached one, by caponnières, or counterscarp galleries. The work is usually organized with a covered-way having one or more casemated redoubts, and a system of mines both for the exterior and interior defence.

**184.** The defensive barrack is usually arranged for two or three tiers of covered fire, and an upper one with an ordinary parapet and terre-plein on which the guns are uncovered and destined for the distant defence. The two upper tiers of covered fire are for artillery, to sweep the interior of the work, and to reach by curvated fires the approaches on the exterior. The lower tier is loop-holed for musketry to sweep the interior. The barrack is surrounded by a narrow ditch on the interior, and this, when necessary, is flanked by small caponnières placed in it, which are entered from the lowest story. The barrack communicates with the interior by a door at some suitable point; and the communication between the interior of the work and the exterior is through doors in the wall enclosing the gorge.

**185.** Considerable diversity is shown in the profiles of these works. They usually consist of a parapet and rampart of ordinary dimensions for the uncovered defence; of scarps either partly detached and loop-holed, with a corridor between them and the parapet; or of scarps with relieving arches arranged with loop-holes for musketry; or of a combination of these two. The height of the barrack, and the command of the parapet of the exterior work, are so determined that the masonry of the former shall be perfectly covered from the direct fire of artillery, and the exterior be perfectly swept by the artillery of the work. The portions of the counterscarps at the salients are also arranged with defensive galleries to sweep the ditches; usually with musketry, but in some cases with artillery.

**186.** Casemates are arranged for mortars in the salient angles of the work, to fire in the direction of the capitals; and one or more casemated traverses are placed on the terre-plein, to obtain a fire on the exterior and to cover the terre-plein from ricochet. The masonry of these traverses is masked by the parapet.

**187.** Posterns lead from the interior of the work to the scarp galleries, the corridors, the ditch caponnières, and the casemated mortar battery in the salient.

**188.** The system of mines for the exterior defence consists simply of listening galleries leading outwards from the counterscarp galleries. That for interior defence is similarly arranged; the communications with it being either from the barrack caponnières, or from the counterscarp of its ditch.

**189.** The work is provided with powder magazines which are placed at the points of the interior least exposed to the enemy's fire; and covered guard-rooms, store-rooms for mining tools, etc., are made in connection with the posterns.

**190.** In the profiles of their works, the German engineers follow nearly the same rules for the forms and dimensions of their parapets as those in general use in other services. They employ three kinds of scarp revetments.

1. The ordinary full revetment, or sustaining wall, with counterforts.

2. Revetments with relieving arches, either with or without defensive dispositions, as circumstances may demand.

3. Scarp walls either partly or wholly detached from the rampart and parapet.

In all these cases, they give to their scarp walls a height from 27 to 30 feet for important works; and about 15 feet for those less so. The batter of these walls is usually one base to twelve perpendicular. For the full revetment with counterforts, they regulate the dimensions of both so as to afford the same stability as in the revetments of Vauban.

In their revetments with simple relieving arches, they use either one or two tiers of arches; placing the single tier either near the top, or towards the middle of the wall, according to the nature of the soil and the pressure to be sustained.

Revetments with relieving arches for defence, or scarp galleries, are arranged for one or two tiers of fire. The back of the gallery is sometimes left open, the earth falling in the natural slope in the rear; or it is enclosed either with a plane or a cylindrical wall, according to the pressure to be sustained.

When the upper part of the wall is detached, to form a corridor between it and the parapet in its rear, the top portion alone is, in some cases, arranged with loop-holes and arcades, or with recesses to their rear, to cover the men from shells; in others, a scarp gallery is made below the floor of the corridor to give two tiers of fire. The corridors are from 8 to 20 feet in width; and when deemed requisite, they are divided, from distance to distance, by transverse loop-holed traverse walls for defence.

When the scarp walls are entirely detached, they are arranged for either one or two tiers of fire, with arcades to cover the men; the banquette tread of the upper tier of loopholes resting on the arches of the lower tier of arcades.

The counterscarps are revetted either with the ordinary wall, or arranged with a defensive gallery with a full centre arch, parallel to the face of the counterscarp wall.

**191.** The German engineers make a liberal use of bomb proof casemates for mortar and gun batteries. The former are either placed in the rear of the parapet, or of the rampart and along the faces; or else in a salient angle.

In the former case, they are covered in front by the parapet; in the latter, either by the scarp wall alone, or by a casemated defensive mask, placed in front of the battery.

When placed along the face (Pl. LXI., Fig. 50), they are arranged for one or several mortars, and frequently with two tiers of arches, the upper one for the service of the mortar, and the lower one for a bomb-proof shelter for troops, or munitions. The chamber occupied by each mortar is a rectangle 12 feet wide and about 20 feet in depth; this is covered by a full centre rampart arch, the height of the piers at the back of the chamber being 4 feet and in front from 6 to 9 feet above the level of the mortar platform. This enables the shell to clear the top of the parapet in front, which is about 12 feet above the level of the platform, and 21 feet in front of the battery.

The chamber is, in some cases, left open both in front and rear, to allow the smoke to escape readily, and to diminish the effect of the concussion of the discharge on the masonry; in other cases it is closed by a wall in the rear; an opening being left in this wall immediately under the arch for the same purpose.

A small ditch is placed in front of the battery; and the wall in front is extended about three feet above the platform, to shelter the men from the explosion of shells that may fall into the ditch.

The abutments of the arches are 7 feet thick and the piers 4 feet. The arches are 2 feet 6 inches thick; they are covered on top by from 4 to 6 feet in thickness of earth; and, in like manner, the arch and abutment are secured on the side exposed to an enfilading fire.

An ordinary traverse is placed on the same side, to cover the masonry and communication between the front of the battery and the parapet; the chambers of the mortars are entered from the front, or from the sheltered side, by a door in the abutment.

When placed in an obtuse salient, behind a scarp with a corridor, a space of 10 or 12 feet is left between the back of the scarp wall and the front of the battery. The platforms of the mortars are about the same distance below the top of the scarp. The arches are covered by the earth of the parapet to the depth of 5 or 6 feet. The dimensions and arrangement of the chambers and arches are the same in this as in the preceding case.

The communication from the interior of the work to the battery is by a postern 6 feet in width. A casemated guard-room is made in connection with the postern; and when the scarp is arranged with relieving arches, either for defence or for other purposes, an arched stairway is in some cases made as a communication from the postern to the casemates. A transversal wall with a doorway serves to cut off the court in front of the battery from the corridor to the rear of the wall.

In the less obtuse salients, the front of the battery is made circular; the chambers being so placed that the fire of the mortars can be thrown in the direction of the capital. A casemated defensive traverse, placed in the salient, masks the battery in front; and it is covered on the flanks by the earth on the top of the arches. The details otherwise are the same as in the preceding case.

**192.** In the arrangement of casemated traverses for guns (Pl. VI., Figs. 48, 49), the chamber for each gun is a rectangle 24 feet in depth, estimated from the interior crest of the parapet, and 12 feet wide. The chamber is covered by a full centre arch, the height from the level of the platform to the crown of the arch being 8½ feet. The arch is 2 feet thick, the piers between the arches 3 feet, and the abutments 3½ feet. The mask wall in front of the chambers is 3 feet thick. This wall is covered in front by the parapet, and by several layers of fascines, or of heavy timber laid across the embrasure in the parapet and above the one through the mask wall. The cheeks of the embrasure in the parapet are likewise revetted with heavy timber at some distance in front of the mask wall. The masonry is covered on top and on the sides with 5 or 6 feet thickness of earth, to secure it from shells and enfilading shot. The casemates are left open to the rear.

In some cases, a blinded battery for a single gun (Pl. VI., Fig. 49), is arranged by enclosing the sides and front of the chamber with walls, and covering it with a layer of heavy timber, supporting two thicknesses of large fascines, covered with a thickness of 5 or 6 feet of earth; the dimensions of the chamber are the same as in the preceding case.

**193.** The caponnières (Pl. VI., Figs. 37, 38), for flanking the main ditch, usually consist of two faces and two casemated flank batteries of two stories each; the lower story being loop-holed for musketry, and the upper pierced for artillery. Each battery consists of several rectangular chambers; each chamber for a single gun being 12 feet wide and 24 feet deep; or of smaller dimensions, according to the calibre of the gun and the kind of carriage on which it is mounted. The upper chambers are covered with bomb-proof arches, the lower one by arches of sufficient strength for the weight thrown upon them. The front mask wall of the casemates is 6 feet thick; the wall in the rear is 3 feet thick and is pierced with windows for light and ventilation. Openings for the escape of the smoke are also made in the front mask wall immediately below the crowns of the arches.

An interior court 30 feet in width is left between the two flank batteries, and when the batteries are detached from the scarp wall the space between is enclosed by a loop-holed wall built on each side in the prolongation of the front mask wall.

The faces of the caponnière form a salient of 60°. They are separated from the flanks by two stories of arched corridors, in front of which are two arched chambers of two stories; the upper chamber being arranged for mortars. An open triangular court is left between the front walls of these chambers and the faces of the caponnière. The upper part of the walls of the faces along this court are arranged with arcades and loop-holed for musketry, and have an open corridor in their rear on the same level as the chambers of the second story.

The caponnière is provided with a powder magazine and other necessary conveniencies for the defence.

The flanks of the caponnière and its interior are swept by the musketry of the scarp galleries in its rear. The faces in like manner are swept by artillery and musketry in casemates behind the scarp.

The arched chambers of the upper story are covered by a thickness of 5 or 6 feet of earth.

**194**. Caponnières of smaller dimensions, termed *bastionnets* (Pl.V., Fig. 39), placed at the angles of redoubts to flank the ditches, are usually arranged for musketry, but sometimes receive artillery. Those for flanking the ditches of the independent works in advance of the enceinte, are sometimes placed in the ditches of these works; sometimes behind the scarp wall of the enceinte; and sometimes in casemates in the main ditch, detached from the scarp wall.

The communications from the interior with the caponnières are by posterns.

**195**. The defensive barracks, forms one of the most distinctive features in the organization of the German fortifications. The plan of these works may be of any figure to suit the object to be subserved by them. When placed in the gorge of an independent work and serving as a keep to it, their plan is usually semicircular.

The barrack consists of one or two stories of arched chambers for covered fire, and an open battery on top with an earthen parapet and terre-plein.

The arched chambers are formed by connecting the front and rear walls of the barrack by transversal walls which serve as piers for the arches of the ceiling, the soffits of which are either cylindrical or conoidal, according as the piers are parallel or otherwise. The chambers are about 18 to 20 feet wide, and 60 feet in depth; their height, under the crown of the arch, from 9 to 11 feet. The arch of the highest chamber is 2½ feet thick, and being covered with a capping and the earth of the open battery on top, is bomb-proof. The arches of the lower stories are 1½ feet thick. The front wall of the barrack is usually 6 feet, and is pierced in each chamber with one embrasure and two loop-holes. The rear wall is 3 feet thick, and has a window in each chamber for light and ventilation. Openings for ventilation are also made in the front wall just beneath the crowns of the arches. Doorways are made through the transversal walls to form a communication between all the chambers. These are sometimes placed along the centre of the piers, at others near their extremities, so that the chambers being divided by slight partitions into two compartments for the quartering of the troops, there will be a continuous hall either along the centre, or near the rear wall, upon which all the apartments open. The barracks are, otherwise, arranged with all the requisites for lodging the troops comfortably and healthfully. The lower story of the barrack is surrounded by a narrow ditch. A drawbridge across this ditch secures the entrance to the barrack at the gorge.

In some cases (Pl. LXXI., Fig. 53), where the front wall of the barrack is much exposed to the besieger's fire, the piers are made thicker near the front wall; and they each have two vertical grooves to receive timber, laid horizontally, between which sand-bags can be packed in to afford shelter when the front wall has become much damaged by the besieger's artillery.

**196. Remarks.** The foregoing summary description, with the plates, will give a good general idea of the principal defensive arrangements constructed of masonry which enter so largely into the recent German fortifications, and upon the details of which the German engineers have bestowed great attention.

The adoption of the polygonal system, with caponnière defences for the main ditch, has enabled the German engineers to give, in their fortifications, a greater exterior side than in the bastioned system generally, and still admit of lines of defence in which grape, canister and small-arms, particularly the later improved musket, will tell with efficacy upon the beseiger's works on the glacis around the salients of the enceinte. With a few exceptions, nothing of a very reliable character has been published as to the plan of these works, further than the general defensive dispositions. From these it appears that, keeping in view the cardinal point in all fortification, the adaptation of the various fronts to the site of the work, so that all the approaches upon them shall be commanded and swept by their fires, whilst the principal lines of the enceinte receive the best direction to place them as little as possible within the range of enfilading positions, the exterior side is usually kept somewhere between 500 and 600 French metres, or between 450 and 700 yards.

## II.

### FRONTS OF POSEN.

**197.** The following is an outline of the plan and defensive dispositions of a front of the fortifications of Posen, one of the most noted of these recent structures.

The exterior side, AB (Pl. XXII., Fig. 2), is 580 yards; a distance, CD $= \frac{1}{15}$ AB, is set off on the perpendicular of the front and within it; and on the line joining the salients A, B with D, distances, AH, BM, equal $\frac{1}{6}$ AB, being set off, give the faces of the front.

The salient, E, of the independent work is on the perpendicular of the front, and at a distance from C equal to $\frac{1}{3}$ AB. Describing from E an arc with a radius of 20 yards, and drawing tangents to it from the points H and M, gives the counterscarps of the independent work; the faces, EF, EF′, are parallel to the counterscarp and equal $\frac{1}{4}$ AB.

The ditches of this work are flanked by casemated caponnières, HI, MN, which are 35 yards in length, or sufficient for four guns; the directions of these flanking casemates being nearly perpendicular to the direction of the faces EF′. The flanks, FG, F′G′, receive the most suitable directions for sweeping the approaches in advance of the salients of the front.

The main ditch is about 30 yards wide, its counterscarp being parallel to the faces of the enceinte; and the gorge of the independent work is on the prolongation of this counterscarp.

The curtains of the enceinte are directed from the points I,

N on the point C, and are thus nearly parallel to the exterior side.

The main ditch is flanked by a large, casemated, defensive barrack, having three stories of covered fire, the lower for musketry and the upper for artillery, and an open battery on top. The plan of this work is that of the letter U; the circular part projects within the independent work, and serves as its keep; the sides are nearly perpendicular to the faces of the enceinte, and are prolonged within the enceinte, serving as a defensive caponnière to flank the main ditch, to sweep the terre-pleins of the enceinte curtains, and also the interior within the range of the guns of two round towers with which the sides are terminated. The sides of the barrack are separated from the rampart of the curtain by lateral ditches 10 yards wide, which give access to the main ditch from the interior for troops in large bodies for sorties.

The parapet of the enceinte (Fig. 4), is thrown back from the scarp, leaving a corridor between the foot of its exterior slope and the scarp wall, the floor of which is 12 feet above the bottom of the main ditch.

The scarp wall rises 16 feet above the level of the floor, thus giving it a total height of 28 feet above the bottom of the main ditch. This wall is loop-holed for small-arms.

The counterscarp wall of the main ditch is 24 feet in height.

The faces and flanks of the enceinte have a relief of 44 feet; the relief of the curtain being only 40 feet.

The corridors of the curtain terminate at the court or open space behind the flanking casemates, HI, MN.

Posterns lead from the interior to the corridors of the faces and flanks, and from the lateral ditches to the corridors of the curtain.

The interior open space between the sides of the defensive barrack is closed by a loop-holed wall between the end towers. A ditch surrounds the towers and the gorge between them, across which a bridge, terminated at the wall by a draw, gives access to the interior open space and the barracks.

**198.** The scarp, rampart and parapet (Fig. 5), of the independent work are arranged with a profile similar to that of the enceinte. The circular portion of the defensive barrack which serves as the keep is surrounded by a ditch, which is swept by small caponnières attached to the keep. A circular mortar battery, covered in front by a casemated traverse, is placed in the angle of this work; and behind this a casemated battery for howitzers is placed on its terre-plein, in the direction of its capital, to give reverse views on the glacis of the collateral independent works. The gorge of this work is closed by a loop-holed wall which extends between the keep and the scarp wall of the flanks.

The communication between the main ditch and the interior is through a gateway in this wall. Posterns lead from the interior to the corridors of the faces and flanks, and to the mortar battery in the salient.

**199.** The counterscarp of the independent work is arranged with a defensive gallery, with which a system of mines for the exterior defence is connected. A system of mines for the exterior defence is connected with the small caponnières in the ditch of the keep.

**200.** The covered-way is without the usual traverses, its interior crest being broken into a crémaillière line. Its salient and reëntering places-of-arms are occupied by casemated redoubts. The communications from the main ditch to the covered-way are by wide ramps which are at the gorges of the reëntering places-of-arms and under the fire of their redoubts.

## III.

### FORT ALEXANDER.

Among the most reliable of the published plans of German fortification is that of the main front of Fort Alexander, a detached quadrilateral work of the fortifications of Coblentz, given by Colonel Humphrey of the British Army.

**201. Plan.** The exterior sides of the enceinte of this fort (Pl. XXII., Fig. 6) form a parallelogram, the acute angles of which are 85°. The main and rear fronts are each 500 yards, and the other two 420 yards each. The main front is of the polygonal system, with a strong defensive caponnière to flank the main ditch.

The caponnière is covered by a demi-lune, and the salients of the enceinte by counterguards; the ditches of these works being flanked by casemated batteries at the reëntering formed between them.

There is no covered-way in front of these outworks, their counterscarps being of earth with a gentle slope. A small earthern work, containing a casemated redoubt, is thrown up at the salients of the counterguard counterscarp.

To construct the traçé take ab=500 yards for the exterior

side of the enciente, which divide into three equal parts, ad=de=eb. Bisect ab by a perpendicular on which set off hH=hd=he=$\frac{1}{6}$ ab. Through H drawing a parallel to ab and setting off along it the distances HA=HB=320 yards, the points A and B will be the salients of the counterguards.

From H, as a centre, with the radii Hd=He, describe two arcs, on which set off from d and e the chords di=ek=33 yards, these will be the lengths of the casemated flanks; ik being joined gives the enceinte curtain.

The salient angle of the main caponnière is constructed by drawing from a point, m, on the capital, at a distance of 20 yards from the lines Hd, He, lines to the extremities i and k of the casemated flanks. The flanks of the caponnière, tn=vo, extend back to the exterior side, and are 33 yards in length and 33 yards apart; or each 16½ yards on each side of the capital.

The faces of the counterguards are directed on the point C=$\frac{1}{12}$ AB=53½ yards on the capital from H.

The salient F, of the demi-lune is $\frac{1}{6}$ AB=106 yards from the point C; its faces FD, FE, are parallel to the lines Hd, He, which last, joined by an arc of a circle described from m as a centre, with a radius of 20 yards, and terminated at the counterscarp of the enceinte ditch, which is 28 yards from ab, will give the demi-lune gorge.

A casemated battery for 3 guns, behind the demi-lune scarp wall, flanks the counterguard ditch; and one for 3 guns flanks the demi-lune ditch, and closes the opening between the demi-lune and counterguard at this point. A narrow ditch 10 feet wide is left between the flank of this battery and the extremity of the counterguard, as a communication between the main ditch and the ditches of the outworks. This opening is masked by an overlap of the counterguard.

Casemated, or blinded, batteries are made in the salients of the enceinte and of the demi-lune.

**202.** The main caponnière (Fig. 8) has two tiers of covered artillery fire on the flanks, of 5 guns each; the lower to sweep the main ditch, the upper the terre-pleins of the counterguards; its faces have two tiers of loop-holes. It has no uncovered fire, but a simple covering of earth as a bomb-proof.

**203.** Casemates, for five mortars each, are placed in the salients of the enceinte at the foot of the rampart slope.

**204.** A narrow corridor (Fig. 6), the floor of which is 20 feet above the bottom of the main ditch, is left behind the scarp wall of the enceinte; the faces and curtains of this wall are loop-holed and arranged with arcades to shelter the men, like the detached scarp walls of Carnot. These scarps are 30 feet high. The height of the enceinte above the parade is 26 feet.

**205.** The scarp walls of the demi-lune and counterguards (Fig. 7), are arranged like those of the enceinte. The command of these works is 16 feet. Their counterscarps are arranged with loop-holed galleries, from which communications lead to a system of mines for exterior and interior defence.

**206.** The rear side of this fort, not being exposed to artillery, is simply closed by a loop-holed wall and ditch. A large, circular, defensive barrack occupies the centre of this rear front, serving as a keep to the fort, and to sweep by its fire the ground on the rear and flanks of the front.

**207. Remarks.** It will be seen that in the arrangement of the plan of this work, the polygonal system, with caponnière defences, of Montalembert, has been adopted as the basis, with such modifications as the features of the site afforded to withdraw the principal lines from the range of enfilading views.

The German engineers apply the preceding dispositions to every class of detached works, whether within reach of the artillery of the main work or beyond it.

In the former case the work is either in the form of a lunette or a redan, according to the requirements of the site; the gorge of the work being secured by a slight loop-holed wall that can be readily destroyed by the artillery of the place; and thus open its interior to view when occupied by the besieger.

In the latter, the plan is that of a polygonal redoubt enclosed on all sides by a parapet.

The ditches in all such cases are flanked by small caponnières, placed at the angles of the work, and arranged both for musketry and artillery; besides having a counterscarp gallery which serves as the point of departure for the galleries of the exterior system of mines.

The apparently wide divergence between the German fortification of the present day and the bastioned system, which last had been adopted as the normal one throughout the world until these innovations were practically introduced, has given rise to active discussions among engineers in Europe, in which, as in all such cases, very ultra ground has been taken by both parties to the dispute.

**208.** In each system the points admitted as essential in all fortification of a permanent character are sought for, viz.:

1. An enceinte secure from escalade and thoroughly flanked by artillery and small-arms.
2. Such an adaptation of the plan of the enceinte to the site as shall secure, as far as practicable, the principal lines from enfilading views.
3. Outworks of sufficient strength in themselves, and of such defensive relations to the enceinte, as to force the besieger to carry them by regular approaches before being able to assault the enceinte.
4. Interior defensive works, or keeps within the assailable points of the enceinte; and also in the outworks first subject to an attack, to give confidence to their garrisons in holding out to the last extremity.
5. The means necessary for an active defence.
6. The use of mines as an auxiliary.
7. The protection of all masonry by earthen masks from the distant batteries of the besieger.

**209.** The only question then is by which of these two systems the object in view is best attained.

In the solution of this question we are met at the outset by the absence of any reliable tests as to the real value of the defensive means adopted in the German system. No place fortified by this mode has yet been subjected to a siege, and nothing can therefore be with certainty stated as to the degree of resistance the peculiar defensive means adopted may be expected to afford.

Many special experiments in breaching scarp walls and casemates, and the results of the more recent sieges, go to show that all structures of masonry, whenever they can be reached by heavy projectiles within effective ranges, whether in view or not, may be greatly damaged if not entirely ruined; and that troops within defensive casemates exposed to such a fire, would be soon driven out of them by the embrasure shots, and their cannon destroyed.

That the flanking caponnières of the enceinte and of the independent works in the German systems are thus exposed and liable to these objections does not admit of a question. Like assertions may be made of the scarps, which are either wholly or partly detached; and of the traverse walls by which the corridors of the enceinte are divided for defence.

The defensive barracks in the gorges of the independent works, and which serve as their réduits, as well as the loop-holed wall by which the gorges of these works are closed, being thrown back from the cover of their parapets, are also similarly exposed.

The German engineers, it is said, have, by the dispositions made in some of their more recent structures, by abandoning the countersloping glacis of Carnot and his detached scarps, employing in their stead, on fronts of attack, scarps with relieving arches, and covering, to some extent, their ditch caponnière defences by earthen masks, shown some distrust of the methods mostly used in their first structures, planned upon the views of Montalembert and Carnot.

**210.** The polygonal traçé which obtains in most of the recent German works has certain prominent advantages and defects which may be seen by a slight comparison with the bastioned system.

As the exterior sides are longer and the reënterings of the enceinte less deep than in the bastioned systems, it follows:

1. That the interior space enclosed by the enceinte is greater in the polygonal traçé.

2. That the faces of the enceinte are less exposed to ricochet from the greater obtuseness of the salient angles.

3. That the fire of the faces has thus a better bearing on the distant defence.

4. That, requiring fewer fronts on a given extent of line to be fortified, there will be fewer flanks and more artillery therefore disposable for the faces and curtains.

5. That, in the usual mode of attack, the besiegers will be forced into a greater development of trenches for the same number of fronts.

**211.** Its defects are:

1. That the enceinte, having no other flanking defence than the main caponnière, will be exposed to an escalade so soon as the fire of this defence is silenced.

2. That the progress of the besiegers during the last and most important period of the siege is but little delayed, owing to the slighter reënterings formed by the independent works in front of the enceinte salients.

**212.** The defects in the bastioned traçé and the modes proposed by different engineers to remedy them, particularly those of Choumara, have been sufficiently dwelt upon to show that, with the advantages inherent in this traçé of preserving the means of flanking the enceinte ditch to the last; of throwing the bastion salients into deep reënterings; and giving a better direction to the enceinte faces for sweeping the ground in advance of the demi-lune salients; it is susceptible of receiving all the means of casemated defences; of a great development of flank fire; of defensive arrangements of mines; of ample communications for an active defence; and an extension of the exterior side fortified commensurate with the improvements of late years in artillery and small-arms.

**213.** In the discussions which have taken place upon the merits of these two traçés, between engineers of the two rival schools, each has seemed disposed to exaggerate the defects, and to depreciate the advantages of the system analyzed, and has conducted his mode of attack accordingly. The true point, however, as to the inherent merits of the question, does not lie in a comparison of the means of resistance of a bastioned traçé with defective communications and without casemated defences and mines with that of the German system, but between the former with these additions, now regarded by engineers of every school as indispensable to a vigorous defence against the greatly improved means of attack of the present day, and the latter.

**214.** The fragility of masonry and the ease with which it can be ruined by distant batteries of heavy calibre, particularly when pierced with embrasures and loop-holes, like the casemated caponnières and defensive barracks of the German system, must naturally incline engineers to limit its employment as much as possible; reserving its use for positions where it will not be subject to this exposure, or where it can be so covered with an earthen mask that nothing may be apprehended from the besieger's heavy guns.

## IV.

### GERMAN FORTS.

**215.** In their detached works or isolated forts, the German engineers follow the same defensive measures as in the independent works belonging to a continuous enceinte.

A strong casemated barrack (Pl. XXII., Fig. 2), the plan of which is either curvilinear or polygonal, with several tiers of fire, serves as the réduit or keep of the work, and is placed either within it or at its gorge, according to the position to be occupied. The interior is provided with casemates, for guns and mortars, placed at the salients and along the terre-plein; frequently under traverses when these are used to cover a face from enfilading views.

The scarp walls are usually built with relieving arches, defensive scarp galleries, and open corridors behind the upper part of the scarp wall, which is also looped-holed. The ditches are flanked by small caponnières, placed at the angles of the work or along its faces, and by looped-holed counterscarp galleries; and mines for exterior and interior defence are connected with these galleries and with the ditch which usually surrounds the keep.

**216. Tower Forts.** The favor with which the views of Montalembert have been received in Germany has led to the adoption of his circular casemated towers, both as isolated forts, and combined in a system of detached works for covering a space to their rear for an intrenched camp, as at Lintz. These towers, in their interior arrangements, are the same as the defensive barrack already described; with the exception of those differences in the details of the construction which the difference in their plans would call for. They have several tiers of covered fire for artillery and musketry, and an open battery on top, the parapet of which is either of earth, or of masonry, according to the dimensions of the tower.

In the towers of Lintz they are surrounded by a ditch, and the whole of the masonry which would be exposed to the besieger's batteries is covered by a glacis, leaving only the guns on top to have direct views on these batteries; the second tier firing under an elevation over the crest of the glacis mask. The ditch towards the interior is crossed by a temporary fixed and a draw bridge leading to the second story of the tower. The guns of the top battery are placed on a revolving platform, their carriages being of a peculiar construction to admit of the axis of the guns remaining parallel, so as not to have their shot diverge from the object to be reached, and, at the same time, to occupy as little space laterally as will just suffice for the service of the guns. An earthen parapet covers the guns on the side exposed to the besieger's fire, and one of masonry towards the interior.

These towers, with the exception of the open battery, have the defects of divergent fires common to all works with a circular plan; and the open battery is liable to be rendered useless, or be ruined by a well-aimed shot or two, or a heavy shell falling on its platform. The tower without earthen masks can only be used with advange in positions where it will not be exposed to being breached from a distance; and is a very good auxiliary in sea-coast defence, for points where the object is solely to prevent an enemy's vessels from making use of a safe anchorage on the coast.

# CHAPTER VI.

## I.

## INFLUENCE OF IRREGULARITIES OF SITE ON THE FORMS AND COMBINATIONS OF THE ELEMENTS OF PERMANENT WORKS.

### SUMMARY.

General conditions (Art. 217).—Conditions of commands (Art. 220).—Adaptation of plan to the site (Art. 221).—Remarks (Art. 223).—Remarks on the defilement of permanent works (Art. 224).—*Data* for the defilement of permanent works (Art. 225)—Limits of defilement (Art. 226).—Dangerous zones of the site (Art. 227).—Portions of zones that may be disregarded (Art. 231).—Defilement of masonry (Art. 232).—Limits of defilement for small works (Art. 233).—Front and lateral limits (Art. 234).—Remarks (Art. 235).—Cases of defilement (Art. 236).—Front defilement of a redan, the command being given (Art. 237).—Reverse defilement of a redan (Art. 238).—Position of traverse for reverse defilement (Art. 239).—Forms and arrangement of traverse (Art. 240).—Combinations of several traverses (Art. 242).—General case of the defilement of a bastion (Art. 245).—Defilement of retired from advanced works (Art. 246).—Defilement by a *parados* (Art. 247).—General remarks (Art. 248).

**217.** Although the same general principles are applicable, and the same conditions must be satisfied in planning a work, so that it shall have all the efficiency of which it is capable, whether the site is unbroken and sensibly horizontal, or presents a great variety of feature, within the range of cannon of the proposed work; still irregular sites, where the surface is of a diversified character, give greater scope for the science and skill of the engineer, and call for all the resources of his art in adapting his plans to the natural features of the site, than level ones.

The principal conditions to be satisfied, and which are the same in all cases, are:

1. That every point exterior to the defences, over which the enemy must approach them, or from which he can annoy them by his fire, should be brought under the fire of the defences.

2. That no point of the defences shall be left unguarded

by their own fire, or present any position where the enemy, obtaining temporary shelter from fire, may gain time to renew an onset.

3. That the troops and *matériel* within the defences shall be sheltered from the enemy's fire in any position he may take exterior to them.

**218.** The problem presented for solution to the engineer in irregular sites is frequently one of no ordinary complexity; demanding a minute and laborious study of the natural features of the position in their relations to the defence; connected with a tentative process of which the object is so to modify the plan, relief and details, ordinarily adopted, as to adapt them in the best manner to the given position. No rules but of a very general character can be laid down for the guidance of the engineer in such cases; among which the following are the most essential, and, when practicable, should be adhered to.

**219.** It has already been observed that, from the means used in the attack by regular approaches, the more plunging the fire of the work, the more efficacious will it prove in retarding the enemy's progress. The efficiency of this fire will depend upon two causes:

1. The command of the work over the point to be attained.

2. The direction of the ground with respect to the lines by which it is swept.

**220.** As to the command of the work over the exterior ground, it has already been shown that motives of economy restrict it, in most cases, within very narrow limits, where, to obtain it, artificial embankments have to be employed.

To augment, therefore, in the greatest degree this element of the defence, advantage should be taken of the natural features of the locality, by placing the principal lines, from which the exterior ground can be seen, on the most commanding points of the site.

If, with this position given to the principal lines, the ground swept falls or slopes towards them, the most favorable combination for an efficacious plunging fire will be obtained; for, with this direction of the ground, the enemy will meet with far greater difficulty, to put himself under shelter by his works, than where the ground falls or slopes from the line by which it is swept; as the surface, in the latter case, descending in the rear of the cover thrown up by the enemy, will be screened to a greater extent than in the former, where it rises in the rear of the cover.

When this, however, cannot be effected, the next best thing to be done is, so to place the principal lines with respect to the surface to be swept that it shall be seen by a part of these lines, thus bringing to bear upon it a flank fire from these parts.

**221.** The general rule, therefore, which the engineer is to take as a guide, in order to satisfy the condition of bringing the exterior ground under an efficacious fire from the work, is:

1. *To place the principal lines of his work on the most commanding points of the site, and in such directions as to bring the exterior ground to be swept in a position sloping towards these lines in such a manner that they can bring their entire fire to bear upon it, or else bring a portion of it to sweep it in front.*

This will generally be best effected by placing the salient points of the work on the most commanding and salient points of the site; as, in this position of the salients, the faces, which are usually the principal lines bearing on the exterior ground, will occupy the salient and commanding portions of the site, whilst the reënterings, being thrown on the reëntering and lower portions of the site, will be in the best position for sweeping the ground immediately in advance of the faces by a flank fire; and at the same time these reënterings will be masked by the faces from the enemy's view, and thus preserved from serious injury up to the moment when their action may be rendered most effective; that is when the enemy, despite the fire from the faces, has succeeded in planting himself upon points on which this fire cannot longer be brought to bear.

To carry these precepts into practice, a wide margin is left to the engineer's judgment, in which he will find it necessary in some cases to extend the lines of his works beyond what a strict regard to economy might prescribe, so as to include within his defences ground from which he can best sweep what is exterior to it, or which, being occupied by the assailant, might make his own position less tenable, in this way forcing him to extend out his lines so as to embrace crests within them that overlook valleys beyond them; and in some cases to throw his own lines further back in order to avoid enfilading or plunging views from points which are too far to be brought within his defences.

2. *The condition of leaving no point of the defences unguarded by the fire*, will depend in a great degree for its fulfilment on the same rule as the preceding. But where

both conditions cannot be satisfied, the distant defence should be sacrificed to the near; as upon the latter the more or less of obstinacy of resistance depends; since the fire of the work and the action of the garrison are the more effective as the point to be guarded is the nearer to the defences.

3. *The condition that the troops and matériel within the defences shall be sheltered from the enemy's fire, from all commanding points without*, will depend upon the relative positions of the principal lines and the exterior commanding points; and as far, therefore, as it can be done, without sacrificing either of the preceding and more important conditions, the plan of the work should be so arranged that the principal lines shall present themselves in the most favorable direction to the exterior ground to avoid plunging, enfilading or reverse views upon their terre-pleins from any point of it.

**222.** To effect these objects, when the work is in the vicinity of commanding heights within cannon range, and the crests of these heights, as seen from the work, present a nearly horizontal outline, the principal lines of the work, fronting the heights, should receive a direction as nearly parallel as practicable to that of the commanding crests.

When the outline of the crests presents a nearly continuous line, but one which declines or slopes towards the site of the work, the principal lines towards the height should receive a direction converging towards the point where the line of the crests, as seen, if prolonged, would join the site.

The reasons for the positions assigned to the principal lines in these cases respectively, may not, at a first glance, be obvious; but by examining the relative positions of the crests of the heights and of the principal lines, as here laid down, it will without difficulty be seen that they can be brought in the same plane, and the latter be so placed as to give a nearly uniform command to the parapets of the principal lines over the site; and that by keeping the terre-pleins of these lines in planes parallel to the one in which the crests of the heights and those of the parapets are held, and at suitable levels below it, the parapets will be made to cover the terre-pleins from the fire of the heights in the simplest manner.

**223. Remarks.** The foregoing general methods for determining the direction of the principal lines fronting commanding heights, so as to cover from direct fire, in the easiest manner, by their parapets, the space to the rear occupied by the troops and *matériel*, present, at the same time, the simplest cases of the adaptation of the plan of a work to the features of the locality, to subserve the object in view. In most cases, all that can be done is to avoid giving such directions to any of the principal lines, as shall be favorable to enfilading or reverse views of the enemy; which may be effected by so placing them that their prolongations shall fall on points where the enemy cannot establish his works; or on those which, if occupied by him, will afford disadvantageous positions for his batteries either for enfilading or reverse fires.

As the attack derives its great advantage from its enveloping position, by which enfilading views and a concentrated fire can be brought to bear on the assailed point, so, in the general disposition of his defences, the engineer should endeavor to reduce these salient and assailable points to the fewest number, and to accumulate upon them such surplus strength that in spite of their natural weakness they will cost the assailant a great deal of time and a large sacrifice of means to get possession.

This consideration has led engineers to propose for the general outline of their defensive polygon a triangle in which the principal development of their work being a number of fronts on a right line, they can neither be enveloped nor their principal lines be enfiladed by the assailant's trenches, thus leaving only the three angular points as assailable, and which they propose to strengthen by an accumulation of works upon them.

Were the engineer untrammelled in all cases by other considerations, this method might do very well. But this is far from being the case. All that he can therefore do in planning his work is to keep this consideration in view, throwing as many fronts as he can on the same right line; making the angles of his general polygon as open as possible, so as to force the assailant to a great development of his works to gain a concentrated and enfilading fire on them; placing these angles on points of difficult access to the assailant; and by taking advantage of such natural obstacles as water and rock, to give additional strength to these points. The skill and judgment of the engineer are here his main reliance in adapting his details to these general principles.

## II.

### DEFILEMENT OF PERMANENT WORKS.

**224. Remarks.** The greater importance of so adapting the plan and command of permanent works to the features of irregular sites as to satisfy the conditions of sweeping thoroughly by their fire all approaches exterior to the defences, and completely flanking the latter, seldom places it in the power of the engineer to fulfil the condition of withdrawing the interior of the defences from either enfilading or reverse views by a modification of either the plan or the command.

To mask therefore the terre-pleins which would be exposed to these fires, as well as from such as would be attained by a plunging fire in front, resort must be had to the usual expedients of defilement; that is, giving to the terre-pleins such positions with respect to their parapets, that the troops and *matériel* upon them will be screened from a plunging fire in front by the parapets; and when the terre-pleins are exposed to either enfilading or reverse views, by so placing earthen traverses or other masks as to intercept these views, and cover the troops, &c., from the enemy's projectiles.

The defilement of permanent works, like that of field works, proposes the same end, and employs nearly the same means. They differ mainly in their practical details; the latter being reduced to a simple practical operation on the field, whilst the former, from the usually greater complexity of the arrangements of permanent defences, requires the aid of mathematical methods, and demands results of extreme accuracy.

**225.** For the solution of all problems of the defilement of permanent works, the engineer requires:

1 The limit exterior to the defences beyond which the effect of the enemy's fire may be regarded as so uncertain as to be neglected.

2. The presumed positions within this limit that the enemy may take up to bring his artillery to bear upon the works.

3. An accurate topographical map of all the ground within the above limits, as given by its horizontal curves referred to a plane of comparison.

4. The magistrals and interior crests of the works, as

either definitely or proximately arranged, referred to the same plane.

**226.** The limits beyond which the enemy's fire, from the usual smooth bore siege guns, may be disregarded, owing to the uncertainty of long ranges, are 1500 yards, where the work is exposed only to a direct, or front fire, and 2000 yards when open to a reverse fire. For rifled guns, which will hereafter be used in all siege operations, these limits should embrace all the exterior ground within the accurate range of the heaviest guns of this class. When the terre-pleins, therefore, are covered, either by their parapets or other means, from batteries at these distances, they may be considered as offering shelters sufficiently secure for the troops, &c., upon them.

**227.** It may happen that there are points beyond these limits, but within the extreme range of siege guns, which, from their positions, it would not be safe to disregard; but these will form exceptional cases, and, when they occur, will be treated in the same manner as those within the limits.

The surface of the site embraced within the exterior limits and the line of defences may be divided into three zones; one lying between the limits and the position of the first parallel of the attack; the second between the positions of the first and second parallels; the third between the positions of the second and third parallels.

In any position that the assailant can take up for his batteries, within the first zone, it is usually estimated that he will not throw up any parapet with a greater command than 10 feet over the ground on which it is placed. Granting this, the muzzles of his guns, behind the parapets, will not be raised higher than 6 feet above the natural surface; so that assuming the surface of this first zone to be raised to 6 feet above its true positon, this may be regarded as the limit, vertically, within which the assailant's lines of fire will be restricted; and therefore if the interior of the defences is covered from the fire within this limit, the troops, &c., will be secure.

That the assailant will not in all likelihood elevate his guns above this limit will seem probable, when it is taken into consideration that any advantage he might derive from doing so would not be commensurate to the labor it would cost him. For, suppose the enemy to have taken up a position for an enfilading battery, at 1000 yards from any salient, to enfilade one of its faces of the length of 100 yards; and that he should decide upon raising his guns 3 feet, or one yard above the limit just laid down; a simple proportion will show that by this increase in the height of his battery he will be able to attain a point at the farther end of the face only 3.6 inches lower than he would have done in the position of the assigned limit, an advantage which, considering the uncertainty of the fire at the assumed ranges, would hardly compensate the additional labor of giving to his works the additional command.

**228.** In the zone between the first and second parallels the limit may be reduced to $4\frac{1}{2}$ feet; for at this distance from the defences their fire is so destructive and certain that the enemy cannot, without great loss of life and time, raise the parapet of his batteries higher than 8 feet above the natural surface.

**229.** From the third zone the musketry of the enemy may be brought to bear upon the defences; and from this position, during sorties from the defences, or at any other opportune moment when their fire is not active, the enemy might mount on the parapet of his trenches, and from there deliver his fire. This would bring his line of fire about 10 feet above the natural surface. The limit, vertically, of this zone may therefore be assumed at 10 feet above the natural surface.

**230.** Taking, for the purpose of illustration, the ranges of smooth bore guns, the limits of the dangerous ground exterior to the line of defences may be marked off on the topographical map of the site (Pl. VII., Fig. 1), by drawing lines concentric with the line connecting the most advanced salients of the defences, and at the respective distances from it of 1500 or 2000 yards (as the fire may be brought to bear on the front or rear), 600 yards, 300 yards, and 60 yards; and then, considering the references of the horizontal curves of the ground, within the zones thus marked off, to be increased 6 feet in the first, $4\frac{1}{2}$ feet in the second, and 10 feet in the third.

**231.** In the defilement of each part separately of the line of defences, those portions alone of these zones should be regarded as dangerous which are embraced within arcs, or other lines drawn at the foregoing distances from the salients, or the faces of the part to be defiled.

It may also happen that, within the limits of dangerous ground for one portion of the line of defences, there may be other portions which, from their position, may mask the portion to be defiled from all the dangerous points beyond them; in which case the points thus shut off need not be regarded, in effecting the operations of defilement.

If, for example (Pl. VII., Fig. 1), the limits of dangerous ground for the demi-lune, A, being marked off, it is found that the demi-lune B masks the demi-line A from all fire that might come from the ground beyond B; then this portion of the zones of danger need not be regarded in defiling A.

To ascertain this point it will be only necessary to conceive a right line to be so moved as to rest in each of its positions upon a point of the interior crest of A and on the one of B; and if this line, in all its positions, passes above the surface of the dangerous zones beyond B, then B will serve as a mask for A.

**232.** All masonry should be covered by earthen masks from the direct view of the heaviest guns within the range at which their fire would prove destructive against it.

**233.** In the defilement of works of limited interior capacity, as, for example, the réduit of the reëntering place-of-arms, the double caponnière, and the like, which are, moreover, not habitually occupied by troops, the extreme limits may be reduced.

**234.** Within the limits of the zones of danger, positions may be found for front, for reverse, and for enfilading fire.

If the two faces, for example, of a work be prolonged to intersect the extreme limit of dangerous ground, the sector which they embrace may be termed *the limits of direct* or *front fire*; since, from every position that can be taken up within this sector, a direct fire alone can be brought to bear upon the two faces.

The two sectors which lie adjacent to this may be termed *the limits of lateral*, or *reverse fire*, since they afford positions from which a reverse fire can be obtained against one of the faces, and a front fire upon the other. It is also only within these last limits that positions for enfilading the terre-pleins of the faces can be obtained.

**235. Remarks.** The problems of defilement which present themselves for solution may embrace one or more of these cases in any example; depending upon the relative positions of the interior crest of the work to be defiled, and of the dangerous ground embraced within the foregoing limits.

In the case of direct fire alone, the terre-pleins can be screened by their parapets. In that of a reverse fire on one face alone, its terre-plein, in some cases, may be screened by a suitable position given to the parapet of the other. Where both are exposed to this fire, one or more traverses must be resorted to as a screen. Against an enfilading fire on one face alone, a portion of the parapet of the other, near the salient, may be a sufficient protection in some cases; but, for the most part, traverses, placed across the terre-plein, will be the only remedy.

## III.

### PROBLEMS OF DEFILEMENT.

**236.** It does not come within the scope of this summary to examine the many cases of defilement which may arise from irregularities in the site. Those alone will be discussed which are of most ordinary occurrence, and which require for their solution the usual geometrical constructions involved in tangent and secant planes and other surfaces to a surface defined by the projection of its horizontal curves. The cases which will here find their application may be arranged under two heads:

1. The plan and command of a work being definitely decided upon, to ascertain the exact portions of the zones of danger, from which any description of fire can be brought to bear upon its terre-pleins, and to defile them from it.

2. The plan of a work being definitely fixed, but its command only approximately within certain limits, to ascertain the easiest method of defiling the terre-pleins of the work, by varying the command, or position of the interior crest, within the assigned limits.

**237.** (Prob. 1, Pl. VII., Fig. 2.) *The command or position of the interior crest of the faces of a work being fixed, to ascertain the dangerous points on the exterior, and to defile its terre-plein from these points.*

Let a b, a c, be the projections of the given crest; and the curves (28.0), (29.0), etc., those of the natural surface.

Prolong outwards to c and d, the faces; construct the scales of declivity of the two lines, a e, a d; and, from them, the scale of declivity, e f, of their plane.

From the salient, a, supposing an arc to be described with a radius of 1500 yards, the dangerous ground will be included between it and the two faces of the work.

Now, if the plane of the interior crests, of which e f is the scale of declivity, be indefinitely extended, and its intersection with the surface parallel to the natural surface and 6 feet above it be found, it is evident that the portion of this raised surface which lies below the plane may be disregarded, as no fire from it can have a plunge upon the interior of the work. But, from every point of the surface above the plane, a plunging fire can be brought to bear on the terre-plein.

Having drawn the horizontals of the plane, e f, and found their intersections with the corresponding horizontals of the raised surface (which last will be given by adding 6 feet or two yards to the references of the curves of the ground), of which x y z is the projection, that portion of the surface which lies above this curve will alone have a plunging fire upon the work, and will be the only portion for which defilement will be necessary.

Now, as this intersection falls entirely within the angle, d a e, of the faces prolonged, or within the limits of front fire, it is evident that the terre-pleins will require to be defiled only from direct fire.

To effect this, let a plane be passed through the face, b a d, of the work, and tangent to the raised surface above x y z. This plane will pass above all the dangerous ground, except at its point of contact with it; and, being extended back from the face within the work, it is clear, if the terre-plein of this face be so taken with respect to this plane that no point of it shall be less than 8 feet below the plane, that then every point of the terre-plein will be screened from a plunging fire by the parapet of the face a b. Now, if the same series of operations be gone through with for the face, c a e, then will its terre-plein be defiled in like manner; and thus the defilement of the whole work be completed for this case.

The tangent planes which satisfy the above conditions are termed *Planes of Direct Defilement;* and they may be defined as *the planes which, passed through the interior crest of a parapet, leave at least* 6 *feet below them, all the dangerous ground of front fire, and pass at least* 8 *feet above every point of the terre-plein behind the parapet.*

The terre-pleins are usually parallel to their respective planes of direct defilement and 8 feet below them. But when the declivity of the plane of defilement exceeds $\frac{1}{25}$, then the terre-plein, if it is to receive cannon, must be kept within this limit.

In the Fig. 2, the references are put down in yards. The tangent plane through b a d is determined in the usual manner, by finding the horizontal (in this case 30.0), among all those drawn to the curves of the raised surface, which makes the minimum angle with b d. The line, h i, perpendicular to this horizontal, is the scale of declivity of this plane; and the point, p, that of contact. The line, k l, is, in like manner, the scale of declivity of the other plane, and o its point of contact.

It might happen, from the steepness of the terre-pleins, that the reëntering or gutter formed at their intersection would be inconvenient, and it would therefore be desirable to have this position raised, when it can be done without exposure to a plunging fire.

This, in most cases, may be effected in this way. It will be seen, from an inspection of the Fig. 2, that the points o and p are the only ones from which the enemy's fire passes exactly at 8 feet above all the points of the respective terre-pleins determined by the tangent planes; and that if, from these points, lines of fire, o a r and p a s, be drawn, every other line of fire through a, from the ground in the angle, p a o, will pass more than 8 feet above the portion of the terre-pleins embraced in the angle, s a r, since the ground within the exterior angle lies below the tangent planes.

If, then, a be taken as the vertex of a cone, the elements of which are tangent to the raised surface within the angle, p a o, and if these elements be prolonged within the work, their prolongation will form a cone of lines of fire, which will pass more than 8 feet above the terre-pleins. If these last, therefore, be connected by a surface parallel to this cone, and 8 feet below it, this surface may be taken as the portion of the terre-plein which, connecting the two plane portions, will remedy the inconvenience pointed out.

**238.** (Prob. 2, Fig. 3). *The data being the same as in the preceding case, and the work being exposed to both direct and reverse views, to cover its interior from these views.*

Suppose the plane of the interior crest of the faces extended within the limits, and its intersection with the dangerous ground determined as in the preceding case; and let x y z, m n o, and p q r, be the curves of this intersection.

The face a b will be exposed to direct fire alone from the ground above the two curves x y z and m n o; and to reverse fire from that above the curve p q r. In like manner, the face a c will be exposed to direct fire from x y z and p q r, and to reverse fire from m n o.

The defilement of each face from the direct fire will be effected precisely in the same way as in the preceding Prob.

The lines h i and k l are the scales of declivity of the planes of direct defilement of the faces respectively.

For the reverse defilement, a plane is passed through a b, tangent to the surface above p q r; and one through a c, tangent to the surface above m n o, and their line of intersection a a′ found. The line u v is the scale of declivity of one of these planes, termed a *Plane of Reverse Defilement* and s t that of the other.

Now, if a traverse is so placed that its crest shall occupy the position of the line a a′, it will cover all between it and the two faces, as high as the interior crests, from the reverse fire on each side. But as it is desirable to have the troops, when on the banquettes, screened from this fire, the crest of the traverse should be raised from 18 inches to 2 feet above the line a a′ to effect this.

The traverse should extend so far towards the gorge of the work that the entire line of each face shall be covered by it. To determine its length with this condition, lines are drawn from the extreme point b and c of the faces, tangent to the curves m n o and p q r, and their points of intersection with a a′ marked; the one that falls farthest from the salient will evidently give the required length.

If the line a a′ should fall so near either of the faces that the traverse, if placed along it, would incommode the service of that part of the work, it will be best to place its crest in the vertical plane a a″ of the capital of the work. When so placed, the intersection of this vertical plane with each of the planes of reverse defilement must be found, and the crest of the traverse be taken 18 inches above the one that lies highest.

**239.** The position of the crest of the traverse, as determined by either of the preceding methods, will be in a vertical plane passing through the salient, a, of the work.

From the thickness and slopes which traverses usually receive, they would ordinarily, if placed in this position, take up all the interior space within the salient, and leave no room there for dispositions either for artillery or musketry. To prevent this, a break is made in the direction of the crest, at some point on the vertical plane through the salient, from which it is directed on a point of either of the faces, so far from the salient that sufficient room will be left for the object in view. In the (Fig. 4), which illustrates this arrangement, the traverse is withdrawn far enough from the salient to leave room for a barbette battery for several guns.

The face upon which the traverse is directed, will be determined by the condition of covering both faces in the most effective manner, by the position taken for the traverse.

**240.** The cross section of traverses for permanent works is similar to those used in field works. The top of the traverse receives a slight slope each way from the crest to the sides. The thickness at top is from 12 to 20 feet to render it shot proof. The sides take the natural slope from the top, either to their intersections with the planes of direct defilement or to the terre-plein. If, to gain interior space, these slopes are terminated at the planes of direct defilement, then the portions of the traverse below these planes are made more steep, and the earth supported by retaining walls. The top of the traverse, where it joins the parapet, being higher than the superior slope, is run out above this slope, upon which the side slopes fall; its extremity terminates in the plane of the exterior slope, extended above the exterior crest.

**241.** Traverses may be arranged for bomb-proof shelters and musketry defence, by throwing a bomb-proof arch between the side retaining walls, and piercing the wall bearing on the portion of the terre-plein which will first fall into the assailant's power with loop-holes.

**242.** When, from any circumstance, a single traverse cannot be used for reverse defilement, resort must be had to several, which should be so combined that no line of fire can penetrate between their extremities to attain any point which they should cover. The examples of like combinations, given in Noizet's method, will readily suggest the manner of making others; of which farther illustration will be found in the following case.

Where a demi-lune is arranged with a réduit, a traverse placed in its salient cannot be extended farther back than the counterscarp of the réduit; and an open space, therefore, will be left at the ditch, through which a reverse fire would attain that portion of either face which is not covered either by the traverse in the salient, or by the parapet of the réduit.

To cover the part thus exposed, it will be necessary to place one or more traverses, which, in combination with the one in the salient, and the parapet of the redoubt, shall subserve this end.

To simplify the case, let the face a c, Pl. VII., Fig 5, be the one exposed, and let the point x be one the fire of which is most dangerous. Having, in the first place, arranged the traverse, t, as in the last example, and drawn the two lines of fire x b and x d, from the point, x, through the extremity of the traverse, and the top of the parapet of the redoubt at the salient, the length, b d, of the face intercepted between these lines will be the part to be covered. If a second traverse, t′, be placed across the terre-plein of the other face of the demi-lune, and in a position such that one of its ends shall rest on x b, and the other on x d, it will evidently cover the portion b d.

**243.** In selecting the positions of several combined traverses, attention must be given to avoid those where, if one be placed, the assailant would find shelter behind it from the fire in the rear. In the example just taken, the slope of t, towards the salient, should be swept by the fire from the rear, through the réduit ditch; the like slope of t′ should be swept by a portion of the réduit face near its salient; and neither so fall as to have the space behind it masked from fire by the one to its rear.

**244. Remarks.** Traverses usually present not only the easiest solution of all problems of reverse and enfilading defilement, but affording the means of rendering the command independent of fire from without, they enable the engineer to regulate this element solely with a view to the effect which he desires to attain by his own fire.

From the space required for their erection, traverses may, as in the cases of narrow terre-pleins, like those of the covered-ways, and of the demi-lune with a redoubt, be inconvenient, both from embarrassing the communications, and from taking up ground that may be wanted for batteries.

**245.** (Prob. 3.) *The plan of a bastion being definitively fixed, and one point of its command approximately, to defile the work in the most advantageous manner, by shifting the position of its interior crest within certain limits.*

Let Fig. 6 be the plan of the work, and a, the salient, the command of which can be varied within certain limits, without impairing any of the other conditions; and let the dangerous ground be embraced within the arc m n, at 1500 yards from a, and the lines a u and a v supposed drawn from a, through covering masses on the right and left of the work.

The front limits of defilement in this case are embraced within the sector m a n; and the lateral limits within the other two m a u and n a v. Now, the most favorable case of defilement here will be that where a plane, containing a, taken within its extreme positions, shall pass above all the exterior ground, and give such a command to the interior crest throughout, when held in it, as shall satisfy the other conditions of defence. To ascertain the existence of such a plane, let a be taken as the vertex of a cone which envelops all the dangerous ground; any plane tangent to this cone will satisfy the condition of defilement, and it will, therefore, only be necessary to find whether any one of these planes of defilement will satisfy the other, of giving the points b, c, d, and e, a suitable command. If no such plane can be obtained, the next most favorable case will be to find one that shall satisfy all the requisite conditions of command, and intersect the ground only within the front limits. In this case it is clear, from the position of this plane, if the interior crests are held in it, that the interior of the work will be exposed only to the direct fire from that portion of the ground which lies above the plane.

Let x y z be the curve of intersection of the plane with the ground, found in the usual way. Through the faces a b and a d, let planes of direct defilement be passed; the terre-plein of the faces being held parallel to them will be covered by their respective parapets from all plunging fire. But, in order that the planes of defilement of the faces shall also defile the flanks, it is necessary that each flank be placed in the plane of defilement of the adjacent face, and its terre-plein in that of the terre-plein of the face. Now, in giving the interior crests of the flanks these new positions, they will lie below the plane that contains the curve, x y z, and in which the interior crests of the faces lie. This being the case, it may happen that the parapet of one of the flanks will not cover the opposite face from reverse fire, coming from the lateral limits opposite the flank. In this contingency, it will be necessary, in order to cover the face, to place the flank in the plane of the curve, x y z, as this plane defiles from the lateral limits; but, in doing this, the flank, d e, for example, will be exposed, in its turn, to the ground above x y z; and to cover it, the only remedy is to erect a traverse, at some suitable point, which shall intercept all this dangerous fire. The least inconvenient position for the traverse will usually be at the shoulder angle. From this point, it must extend so far back as to intercept all fire from above x y z, both on the terre-pleins of the flank and curtain, where they unite, and be high enough to screen the troops on the banquette.

If the defilement cannot be effected by either of these processes, there remains no other means than, having first definitely fixed the command, to divide the bastion by a traverse, either along its capital, or some other convenient direction, and, having given it a suitable height, to cover each portion from direct fire by the usual method.

**246.** The foregoing problems embrace in their solution all of the more ordinary cases of defilement, and suggest the route to be followed in treating others.

In all cases of the defilement of combined works, like the enceinte and its outworks, etc., it must be borne in mind that the advanced works, which, from their position, must first fall into the assailant's power, become thus a portion of the dangerous ground for the works more retired, and which must also be held after the fall of the others. The retired works, under such circumstances, must be defiled from the advanced; their planes of defilement being made to pass from 3 feet to 4.5 feet above the portion of the advanced work on which it is presumed the assailant may make a lodgment, and which, from its position, may be regarded as the most dangerous to the retired work.

It is according to this rule that the réduit of the reëntering place-of-arms is defiled from the parapets of the two adjacent demi-lunes; its plane of defilement extended outwards, passing at 3 feet above the salients of these works.

The tenaille, in like manner, is defiled from the upper terre plein of the demi-lune réduit, as the tenaille must be held after the enemy has established himself on this terre-plein. For like reasons, the more retired portions of the covered-ways are defiled from the enemy's lodgments on the glacis of the demi-lune salient place-of-arms.

**247.** Where a work has considerable command, and is open at the gorge, like the cavalier retrenchments, for example, and the works in its rear do not mask its interior from reverse fire, it may be necessary to place the traverse, termed a *parados*, across its terre-plein at the gorge, giving it sufficient height to subserve the end in view.

**248. General Remarks.** The methods of defilement here laid down are those now followed by engineers. They unite mathematical accuracy in results with great simplicity of detail; and render the defilement altogether secondary to the other conditions of defence, upon which the plan and command are made essentially to depend.

Before they were adopted, the results of the method then followed were, in most respects, like those obtained in the practical operations for defiling field works. A line was taken, the position of which was determined by a series of trials, having for their object to obtain the most satisfactory results both as to the economy of the requisite embankments and the best disposition of command of the various parts at, or in the rear of, the gorge of the work to be defiled; this position coinciding with the natural surface, or being above or beneath it as the case required. Through this line a plane was passed tangent to the dangerous ground. This plane, termed, as in field defilement, a *Rampant Plane*, was taken as the artificial site of the work, in reference to which the relative command of all the parts was arranged as upon a horizontal site. Or, in other words, the result was nearly the same as if the works had been arranged on a horizontal site, and then the whole combination turned around some fixed line of this site, until it was brought into the position of the required rampant plane. The defects of this method are evident at a glance. It preserves the relations of defence of the various works the same as in a horizontal site; but it, to a great extent, leaves out of consideration the bearing of the command on the exterior ground, and, in many cases, may lead to excessive excavations and embankments which the methods now followed enable the engineer, for the most part, to avoid.

In the preceding discussions it will be observed that the limits of defilement, *horizontally*, have been based upon the range and presumed accuracy of fire of artillery and small-arms before the changes which, within a few years back, have taken place in both these particulars, and which --from the zeal and intelligence with which experiments are now being carried on in every part of the civilized world, on the forms of cannon and projectiles and the quality of powder—will, in all probability, be extended and lead to still more remarkable results. These improvements, however, will have no other effect upon the rules and modes of defilement now in use than to change the limits *horizontally*, to correspond with the increased ranges of projectiles. So far as an improvement in the accuracy of fire is concerned, it will render a strict defilement of all parts of the interior of a work more imperative, and will lead engineers to resort to every means by which the troops and *matériel* can be hidden from an assailants view within the extreme range of projectiles. As to the *vertical* limits, there would seem to be no good reason for changing those now established. When it is also taken into consideration that the relative command of heights decreases with their distance from the work defiled, and also that the accuracy of aim is greatly affected by the same cause, it is questionable whether any marked extension of the limits hitherto laid down will be necessary except in special cases of locality of prominent natural features.

Considering that the trajectories of the projectiles are more or less curved lines, depending upon the angles of elevation under which they are fired, and the distance from which they are thrown, it is obvious that when the distances or the angles of elevation are at all considerable, the projectiles, in the descending branch of their flight, will approach more or less a vertical line; and that even in striking the interior crest of a parapet or traverse, they will land on the terre-plein behind, but at a short distance from it.

Defilement from such fire can therefore be only a palliative, screening the interior of the work only from sight; still, even this advantage should be sought for whenever it can be had at not too great a cost.

It is chiefly in the near defence, where the trajectories approach more nearly to right lines, that defilement subserves more completely its purpose of screening from fire the interior of the work.

# CHAPTER VII.

## ACCESSORY MEANS OF DEFENCE.

### SUMMARY.

Water as an accessory (Art. 249).—Marshy sites (Art. 250).—Artificial inundations (Art. 251).—Water applied as an active means of defence (Art 252).—Natural and artificial beds of rock as an accessory (Art. 253).—Stumps of trees as an obstruction (Art. 254).—Mines as an accessory (Art. 255).

## I.

**249.** Water may be made a very important accessory means of defence in many localities—as in a flat, marshy country, where the level of the natural surface lies but at a slight elevation above the water-level; or as, in the case of an undulating surface, where small streams, running through valleys, can be dammed back, so as to produce an inundation of some extent.

**250.** In the former case, the defensive works can be easily girdled by a zone of marshy ground, which will give an assailant great trouble to construct his trenches and other siege-works upon, whilst the work itself can be secured from attempts at surprise, by keeping its ditches filled with water to the depth of six feet at least. In such a locality—moreover, if in a climate where the winters are mild—revetted scarps and counterscarps, the chief use of which is to prevent an attempt at open assault, may be replaced by earthen ones, a strong stockade being formed along a wide berm, answering as a corridor, to give greater security on the more exposed fronts of the work.

**251.** In the latter case, portions of the ground, in the immediate vicinity of the works, may be covered by a sheet of water, of sufficient depth to prevent their being used by the assailant in his approaches; and within the inundation thus artificially produced detached works may be erected, which, by taking flank and reverse views over other lines of approach of the assailant, may force him to make his approach upon other points which will have been strongly fortified to meet this condition of things.

To form these artificial inundations the locality must lend itself to the construction of dams, in such a position that they cannot be reached by the assailant's missiles, and will be secure from any other means he may take to destroy them. This supposes, then, that the stream should either run through the works, so that the dam could be erected within them, or so near to them, that, in combination with some advanced work, the dam may be made secure.

In a locality having these features, the inundation would, as a general rule, have to be formed on the upstream side of the work, since, if made below it, the dam would have to be placed further from the work, and the inundation itself might spread up too far within. Besides these objections to this position, an assailant would evidently have greater facilities for tapping the inundation and running the water off than when it occupies the upstream position.

The position and extent of the dams, and the other necessary constructions connected with them, as sluices, waste weirs, &c., will depend entirely upon the local features of the site, and will form a particular study in each case for the engineer.

**252.** Besides these uses of water as a passive obstruction, arrangements may be made, when the locality is favorable to it, for producing a powerful current to sweep away the assailant's works in the ditches by letting loose a large body of water, which has been dammed back for the purpose, with a rush into the ditches. This, in like manner, will require the same constructions as in the preceding case, and flash gates which can be suddenly turned about a horizontal or a vertical axis, so as to give an outlet to the water in considerable volume and with great velocity. These gates have to be placed in some very secure point of the ditches, inaccessible to the assailant and covered from his missiles, and, if effectively used, may prove a source of great annoyance to him by frequently frustrating his attempts to make a passage of the ditch.

## II.

**253.** Solid hard rock, or even thin layers of soft rock alternating with layers of soil, as was the case at Sebastopol, are great obstructions to an assailant's siege works, as the rock has, in many cases, to be blasted out to gain partial cover, and a large amount of earth, with trench materials, has to be brought forward at great risk of life to form the parapets.

In constructing a work, nothing should be omitted which, if placed on the line of the assailant's approaches, will delay his operations and force him to greater efforts and exposure. To this end, where fragments of rock can be readily had in sufficient quantities, it should be used in forming the embankments of the glacis, and also be thrown in upon other points, over which important lines of trenches must necessarily be run.

Besides these accessory means of delaying the progress of the besiegers' works, a site of solid rock offers the farther advantage of giving natural scarps and counterscarps, where the ditches are excavated out of the rock, of far greater resistance to the assailant's means of destruction than any masonry, however solidly and carefully constructed, can offer; besides forcing the assailant to construct galleries through the rock to attain the level of the bottom of the ditch where his passage of it is to be constructed.

**254.** With a similar purpose, the stumps of large trees may be left in like positions, and trees may be planted when the work is constructed with the object of cutting them down and leaving their stumps when the work is threatened with a siege.

## III.

**255.** Mines, when properly arranged and well played, are so important a defensive means that they should constitute a part of the permanent dispositions of defence of every work where the character of the soil will admit of it, at least on those points which are otherwise weakest, and therefore most liable to be assailed.

As the general arrangement of a combination of galleries and mine chambers, as well as the details for their construction, has already been given, nothing further is called for here than to state that the principal galleries of the combination should be constructed with the work, and of durable materials, leaving the other parts to be done when the exigency calling for them may happen.

# CHAPTER VIII.

## THE DEFENSIVE ORGANIZATION OF FRONTIERS WITH PERMANENT FORTIFICATIONS.

### SUMMARY.

Opinions held by prominent military authorities on the necessity of fortified frontiers (Art. 256).—Remarks on arbitrary systems of frontier defences (Art. 257).—Remarks on the organization of the frontier defences of the United States (Art. 258).—Important points to be fortified (Art. 259).—Rivers and mountain ranges as natural defensive lines (Art. 260).—Advantages offered both in defensive and offensive operations by fortified points on rivers (Art. 261).—Points to be fortified in mountain ranges (Art. 262).—Defensive means adopted for the coasts of the United States (Art. 263).—Character of the works necessary for sea-coast defences (Art. 264).—Defences for important commercial marts and naval depots (Art. 265).—Defences of important extensive roadsteads (Art. 266).—Opinions entertained by foreign military authorities on the fortification in a permanent manner of important inland centres of population (Art. 267).—Fortifications of Paris and Lyons in France (Art. 268).—Objections to the adoption of European practice for the defences of the large cities of the United States (Art. 269).

**256.** No state, in the present condition of civilization, can be regarded as secure from foreign military aggression, the accessible points of whose frontiers are not occupied by permanent fortifications of such strength as shall prevent an enemy from obtaining possession of them by a sudden assault, and thus procuring the means of penetrating into the interior. Guided by the experience of centuries of wars, and the daily increasing facilities which the improvement in the *matériel* of armies and their transportation afford for rapid and powerful offensive operations, the ruling states of Continental Europe have, within the last half century, not only made every effort to place their frontiers in an unassailable condition, but also their great centres of population and wealth in the interior, beyond the chances of a sudden attack from an enemy who might force his way through the frontier defences and march rapidly upon them, thus making these positions the rallying-points where a defeated army can find a safe resting-place until it can be reorganized and sufficiently strengthened to resume the offensive.

Such seems to be the result at which the generals and statesmen of Europe have arrived, after the most mature and careful consideration of the important problem of national defence; at a time when *the utility of permanent fortifications was seriously called in question*, by some who pointed, in support of their views, to the very inefficient part the great number of fortified places had played in the wars waged by Napoleon, when by means of overwhelming numbers in the field, he was enabled to disregard such places, the garrisons of which were too feeble to make any efficient offensive movements, until the defeat of his adversary, in one or more great pitched battles, necessarily also threw them into his possession.

In view of the arguments based on these events, the opinions of Napoleon himself should carry great weight. In speaking of the bearing of permanent fortifications in a defensive war, he says: "If fortresses can neither secure a victory, nor arrest the progress of a conquering enemy, they can at least retard it, and thus give to the defensive the means of gaining time—a most important advantage in all warfare." In like manner the Archduke Charles of Austria, who showed himself one of the ablest adversaries with whom Napoleon was called upon to cope, takes the ground: "That a defensive warfare cannot be systematically and successfully carried on in a country which is not provided with fortresses that have been planned and distributed according to strategical requirements." Like views were held by the Duke of Wellington; and it is probable that no great general, from the earliest period of military operations down to the present moment, has ever entertained the contrary.

Without going further back than the two great contests which have taken place in Europe during the last few years, we gather the strongest testimony to the soundness of these views. We find, on the one side, the efforts of powerful Russian forces paralysed by the obstinate defence of a few weak fortresses, and, in some cases, of simple field works, by the Turks; on the other, the gigantic armaments, by sea and land, of France and England combined, held at bay in the East and in the Black Sea; and more lately the career of France arrested in the very flush of victory by the time which it must necessarily have cost her to break down the barriers which Austria had placed in her way in the strongholds of Northern Italy. The only question then on this subject that remains for solution by a state is in what way such a means of security from aggression can be best adapted to its own geographical, political, and military status.

**257.** Military engineers, and other writers on this branch of the military art, have proposed systems of defensive lines for retarding an assailant at the frontier, of a more or less complicated character; the point aimed at in all cases being to make the works of each line of sufficient strength to defy an open assault even when their garrisons are reduced to their least number, and to combine this obstacle with the active effort of an army holding the open field, and manœuvring in connection with the fortified points, to threaten the flanks and rear of an invading force that might attempt to force its way through the defensive lines without carrying some of the works by a siege.

Although hypothetical cases of this character do very well to hang an argument upon, they are of little practical use, as the points that must necessarily be fortified will be those which lie upon the main avenues of access to the interior from the frontier; as upon these also must lie the principal centres of population from the frontier to the interior. The problem in each case will be therefore a special one, and must be treated upon its own data.

**258.** In a country like our own, with so vast an extent of sea-coast and inland frontier, and with political and social institutions which are so antagonistic to every approach to a large standing army as a measure of national safety, this question is one of peculiar importance, both from the open character of this extensive frontier, and from the almost incredible facility with which, as shown in the late struggle in Europe, and in the contests in China and India, considerable armies, with all their *matériel*, can be concentrated on distant points by the aid of steam. The weakness of our immediate neighbors on the one side, and the daily increasing mutual commercial interests between us and the greatest naval power in the world, by which we might be seriously threatened both along our seaboard and our extensive line of inland frontier, it is true, would seem to favor the hope that the day is still remote, and, from present appearances, may never arrive, in which our country will have to apprehend anything in the shape of invasion except along the sea-coast; and we may, therefore, dismiss from our consideration any other provision against this eventuality (which, should it happen, looking to our resources in men and means, will hardly extend inland beyond a few marches), except what we have already attempted—viz. the securing of our principal harbors, naval stations, and commercial marts from a naval attack, or from one combined with the operations of a land force, which, from the causes above alluded to, could be but of short duration.

**259.** In the organization of the inland frontier fortifications of a state, the points to be principally regarded are the principal avenues of access to it, and their topographical features as they lend themselves more or less to strengthen the artificial defences. In conducting an invasion across an inland frontier, the march of the enemy must necessarily be along the roads that intersect it, as these afford the only means for transporting the *matériel*, etc., of the army. The points, therefore, or places in their neighborhood where the principal roads or other avenues of communication cross the frontier, particularly those which lead to the great centres of population and wealth, are the ones which would necessarily call for permanent defences. No absolute rule can be laid down for the distribution and strength of such works along a frontier. Everything must depend upon the more or less of facility presented to an enemy for penetrating at one point rather than another, and of the ulterior advantages the one may present to him over another.

**260.** Rivers and mountain ranges are the natural fortifications of states; and where they form the frontiers they greatly facilitate the application of artificial defensive means, as they present but few, and those in general important, points of access.

When these points on a river are fortified, an invading force, however powerful, cannot, without great risk, cross the river without first gaining possession of them; for, even should a sufficient detachment be left to observe and blockade the fortresses, the main army, in case of retreat or any disaster, might be placed in an extremely critical position, in its movements to recross the river, with the garrisons of the fortresses threatening its flanks and rear.

**261.** In offensive operations fortresses upon a river frontier form one of the strongest bases of operations. If a river intersects the frontier, the point where it crosses it, or some one in its vicinity should be occupied by a permanent work; among such points those are more peculiarly necessary to be held where a river forming the frontier is intersected by another navigable one which lies wholly within the frontier.

The importance of thoroughly occupying such points is

obvious, as they afford an army on the defensive the means of passing readily and safely from one side to the other of the river, either to evade a force too powerful for it to cope with in the open field, or when an opportunity offers, from any imprudent movement of an invading force on one side, to throw itself suddenly from the other on its flank or rear, and thus forcing it to a retrograde movement.

**262.** With respect to mountain passes, the main roads alone will require permanent works. If the passes are independent of each other, a work will be necessary for each one separately; but where several unite at the same point, upon or within the frontier, a single work placed upon this point will suffice. Local circumstances will determine the point in each pass which, occupied, will offer the greatest advantage for obstructing the march of an invading force and retarding the bringing forward its *matériel*. The only rule that can be given is that, whilst the position selected shall satisfy these conditions, there shall be every facility of communication between the fortress and the interior for receiving supplies and reinforcements. This rule would lead generally to the selection of some point of the outlet within the frontier as the proper one.

**263.** The number of fine natural harbors and roadsteads on our seaboard, where the largest fleets can find a secure anchorage at all seasons; the proximity to the ocean of many of our most important cities, towns, and populous villages, by which they are not only exposed to the usual dangers of naval attacks, but to incursions from an enemy's land forces; together with the large rivers which, having their outlets on this seaboard frontier, are navigable for long distances within it by vessels of the greatest burden—have given to the subject of sea-coast defences a particular prominence among ourselves.

The means of defence disposable for the security of such points consists in permanent works arranged to meet an attack both by sea and land, and of such strength as the presumed nature of the attack will demand; of such temporary fortifications as the exigency of the moment may point out; of movable land forces; and of floating defences to act in aid of the others.

**264.** The character of the permanent defences will depend upon the object in view. Where this is simply to exclude an enemy's fleet from the use of a harbor or roadstead, which offers to him no other inducement for its occupation but that afforded by a secure anchorage, one or more small works of sufficient strength to prevent the success of an open assault upon them, armed with heavy mortars and guns with long ranges, that can reach by their fire every point where an enemy's ship could safely anchor, will be sufficient.

The points to be occupied by these works, as well as their plan, will depend upon the natural features of the harbor or roadstead itself.

They will usually consist either of open works with guns in barbette and mortars sweeping all points of approach to and within the harbor; or of a combination of casemated and barbette batteries; the gorge or rear of the works being occupied by a casemated tower, of sufficient strength and capacity to hold the garrison necessary to beat off an open assault on the battery by land, and be secure from a *coup-de-main*.

Like defences will also be sufficient for the security of the smaller classes of towns and villages which would probably offer a temptation only to a small naval force.

**265.** In the case of important commercial cities and large naval depôts lying within harbors more or less accessible both to sea and land attacks, the character of the defences called for must necessarily be commensurate with the magnitude of the interests to be guarded, and the consequent temptation to an enemy to put forth great efforts for their occupation and destruction.

The avenues of approach to these objects by sea, which can be brought within range of cannon and mortars in fortifications on the shore, or in casemated works erected on natural or artificial islands, should be occupied to a distance that will prevent a fleet from approaching near enough to open a bombardment, and if practicable also force the enemy, if he ventures a land attack, to disembark his forces either at so great a distance from the object to be reached that he will not be able, by a sudden movement of this nature, to effect a surprise; or to limit his landing to such points on the coast as, from their exposed position, may render the coöperation of the naval and land forces very uncertain, and, in case of a storm, place the latter in a very perilous condition if attacked.

These works will form the exterior chain of the defences. Within these, batteries either open or casemated, as the locality may seem to demand, should occupy all the most suitable positions for sweeping the path that a fleet must follow by powerful cross, direct, and enfilading fires, and for reaching every point of anchorage within the harbor.

On the land approaches, points should be occupied by forts of a permanent character, which will prevent a sufficiently near approach to bombard the city or depôt, and, in combination with temporary works, will afford an intrenched field of battle for the troops on the defensive. These will form the exterior line of the land defences, the interior line being either a continuous enceinte of permanent fortification, which will require a regular siege for its reduction, or else a suitable combination of either continuous or detached field works of such strength and armament that the enemy, in any attempt to carry them by an open assault, will be made to suffer heavily even if he is not repulsed.

The security of objects of this character will be greatly increased when they lie at some distance within the seacoast frontier, and can only be approached by water through such comparatively narrow defiles as even our largest rivers present, and by land after one or more marches. These defiles will, for the most part, not only present admirable positions on their banks, from which an assailant's fleet can be enfiladed within the range of the heaviest guns, but frequently others, at points where the river narrows, or changes its course, where works occupying the opposite banks will give the means of rendering the river impassable by torpedoes, booms, rafts, or other floating and sunken obstructions, which cannot be removed except by getting possession of the defences, by which they are guarded, by a land attack.

**266**. Wherever harbors or bays are of that extent that their entrance cannot be interdicted to an enemy's fleet, nor secure anchorage within them be prevented, of which we have examples on our own coast, the case falls beyond the province of fortification, and must be left to floating defences for a solution. Here even some fortified harbors on the shores of such extensive estuaries may give secure places of refuge for ships-of-war, from which they may at any moment sally when they can take the enemy at a disadvantage, or into which they can retreat if attacked by a superior force.

**267**. In the great military states of continental Europe, the question as to what extent the great centres of population and wealth in the *interior* should be covered by fortifications, has been submitted to the investigation of the ablest engineers and statesmen, from the time of Vauban down to the present day. But more particularly since the fall of Napoleon, a catastrophe which might not have taken place had Paris been secured by fortifications which would have prevented a *coup-de-main*, when the armies of the Allies gained possession of it as the result of a pitched battle. Whatever differences of opinion have been called forth as to the mode of accomplishing this object, as shown in the published views on the proposition to fortify Paris, there seems to have been none among those best qualified to decide upon it as to the great importance of so fortifying this capital and other large places in the interior, as Lyons, etc., which from their position must be of the highest strategical value in the case of a successful invasion by a large army, as not only to prevent their wealth and resources from falling into the possession of the invading force, but to make them safe rallying-points for beaten and dispersed forces, and depôts for organizing new armies.

The plan that has been adopted for this end, both in France and in most of the other cities of Europe which have been either newly fortified or had their old works strengthened within this period, is to surround the city by a continuous enceinte of greater or less strength, but one secure from a *coup-de-main*, and to occupy with forts of a permanent character the most suitable points in advance of the enceinte, to prevent an enemy from bombarding the city, or penetrating between them without first gaining possession of them. By this plan, it is proposed to gain all the advantages offered by the passive resistance of fortifications and the activity of a disposable movable force occupying the zone between the enceinte and the forts as an intrenched camp, upon which the forts with temporary works thrown up between them would render an open assault too perilous to be attempted.

**268.** The fortifications of Paris consist of a continuous bastioned enceinte, without outworks, consisting of a revetted scarp of the usual height, to secure it from escalade, and a ditch with a counterscarp of earth. The advanced forts are either quadrangular or pentagonal bastioned works, inclosing all the means of security for their garrisons, as bomb-proofs, etc., their plan being skilfully adapted to the site, and their mutual bearing on the defence. Those of Lyons present more diversity, both in the plan and details of the enceinte and forts; although the general system is the same as that of Paris. There is here seen a more extensive application of casemated and gallery defenses, both for exterior flanking and the defence of the interior forts, growing out of the more broken features of the site generally, and frequently the more confined space occupied by them.

In Germany the same general system of a continuous enceinte, with strong advanced isolated works, has been followed; the whole being so planned and combined as to meet the distinctive features of what is known as the German system of fortification.

**269.** In our own country, where our largest centres of population and wealth lie almost immediately upon the sea-board, it would seem impracticable, in view of the rapid spread of population around them, and the consequent changes in local features, to resort to any defences of a permanent character to secure them from a land attack, even were the nation willing to assume the burden of the great outlay for such an object; as, in a few years, the works of to-day might be rendered useless by the changes referred to. Even in Europe, the strongest despotic governments have been obliged to cede what seemed military exigencies to the demands of the social condition; and either to raze the fortifications of cities, to give room to a crowded population, or else to suffer such encroachments on the ground necessary for their action as to render them nearly useless. The only defensive resource that seems left to ourselves, in like cases, is in the use of field-works—one which our military experience shows may be relied upon with confidence, so long as the military aptitude of our population remains unchanged from what it has thus far proved itself to be.

# CHAPTER IX.

## SUMMARY OF THE PROGRESS AND CHANGES OF FORTIFICATION.

### SUMMARY.

Fortification as seen in its earliest stages (Art. 270).—Enclosures of simple stone walls and towers (Art. 271).—Insufficiency of simple walls and towers against improved means of offence (Art. 272).—Introduction of ditches and wide ramparts as defensive features (Art. 273).—Examples of the great strength and extent of some ancient fortifications (Art. 274).—Methods of attack used by the Ancients (Art. 275).—Defensive measures employed by the Ancients (Art. 276).—Rise and fall of the art under the Romans (Art. 277).—Progress of the art under the Western Empire (Art. 278).—Condition of the art under the Feudal System (Art. 279).—Castellated fortifications of the Feudal Period (Art. 280).—Fortifications of cities during the same period (Art. 281).—Changes in the art occasioned by the invention of gunpowder (Art. 282).—First appearance of the bastioned system and the changes consequent upon it (Art. 283).—Italian school of engineers (Art. 284).—Spanish school (Art. 285).—Dutch school (Art. 286).—German school (Art. 287).—Swedish school (Art. 288).—French school (Art. 289).—Methods and progress of the attack from the invention of gunpowder to the time of Vauban (Art. 290).—Changes and improvements made in the methods of attack by Vauban (Art. 291).—Remarks on the present general condition of the art (Art. 292).—Present condition of the art in the United States (Art. 293).

### I.

**270.** The records of history and the vestiges of remote civilization show that the art of fortification, in some guise or another, has been in practice throughout all nations, even in the lowest stages of social progress, and that, wherever it has been cultivated, its character has been more or less influenced not only by the natural features of the country, but by the political and social conditions of its inhabitants.

In its earliest applications, we find men resorting to one or more simple enclosures of earthen walls; or of these surmounted by stakes placed in juxtaposition; or of stakes alone firmly planted in the ground, with a strong wattling between them; or of timber in its natural state, having its branches and the undergrowth strongly interlaced to form an impervious obstruction, with tortuous paths through it only known to the defenders.

A resort to such feeble means shows not only a very low state of this branch of the military art, but also of that of the attack; as defences of this kind would present but a slight obstacle, except against an enemy whose habitual mode of warfare was as cavalry, or of one not yet conversant with the ordinary plans for scaling. This class of fortifications for the defence of entire frontiers has been mostly met with in the east of Europe, and was doubtless, at the time, found to be a sufficient protection against those nomadic tribes that for ages have roamed over its vast plains, and who are only formidable as a mounted force.

**271.** The next obvious, and, in humid countries, necessary step, was to form walls either of rough blocks of stone alone, or of these interlaced with the trunks of heavy trees. Obstructions of this kind could only be used to a limited extent, and were confined to the defences of places forming the early centres of population. As human invention was developed, these, in their turn, were found to present no serious obstacle to an assault by escalade; giving to the assailed only the temporary advantage of a more commanding position; and they gave place to walls of dressed stone, or brick, whose height and perpendicular face alike bade defiance to individual attempts to climb them, or the combined effort of an escalade. From the tops of these inaccessible heights, sheltered in front by a parapet of stone, and, in some cases, by a covered corridor behind them, the assailed could readily keep at bay any enemy, so long as he could be attained by their missiles; but having reached the foot of the wall, he here found shelter from these, and, by procuring any cover that would protect him from objects thrown from above, could securely work at effecting a breach by mining. It was probably to remedy this defect of simple walls that towers, which at first were nothing more than square or semicircular projections built, from distance to distance, in the wall itself, were first devised; and which subsequently were not only enclosed throughout, but divided into stories, each of which was provided with loop-holes, to flank the adjacent towers and the straight portions of the wall between them. Each tower could be isolated from the straight portion of the walls adjacent to it, by an interruption at the top of the wall, over which a communication between the tower and wall could be established by a temporary bridge.

**272.** These formidable defences were, in their turn, found to be insufficient against the ingenuity and skill of the assailant, who, by means of covered galleries of timber, sometimes above ground and sometimes beneath, gradually won his way to the foot of the wall, where, by breaking his way through it, or by undermining and supporting it on timber props to be subsequently destroyed by fire, he removed the sole obstruction to a bodily collision with the assailed.

These methods of assault were in some cases supported by means of high mounds of earth which were raised in an inclined plane towards the walls, and sometimes carried forward to them, from the top of which the assailant, by the erection of wooden towers, covered with raw hides to secure them from being burnt, could command the interior, and, driving the assailed from the walls, gain a foothold on them by lowering a drawbridge from the wooden tower.

**273.** These changes in the attack led to new modifications in the defence, which consisted in surrounding the place by wide and deep ditches, of which the walls formed the scarp, the counterscarp being either of earth or revetted. This placed a formidable obstacle to the mode of attack by mining, and also to the use of earthen mounds, as these last had to be constructed across the ditch before they could gain sufficient proximity to the wall either to form a communication with its top, or to breach it by means of the battering-ram; the ditches also were filled with water whenever this obstruction could be procured, and when dry they formed a defile through which the assailed often sallied upon the assailant with success when found at a disadvantage in it.

**274.** The gigantic profile often given to the fortifications of antiquity seems almost incredible, as well as their extent. In many cases a double wall of stone or brick was filled in between with earth, forming a wide rampart upon which several vehicles could go abreast. Not only was the space enclosed by some of these fortifications that requisite for the habitations, but ground enough was taken in to add considerably to the food of the inhabitants and cattle, for the long periods to which blockades were in many cases extended, when all other means of reducing the place had failed.

The wall built by the Romans, between Carlisle and Newcastle, to restrain the incursions of the Picts into the southern portions of the island, was sixteen miles in extent, about twelve feet in height, and nine feet in thickness. The extent and dimensions of this work sink almost into insignificance when compared with those of the celebrated wall of China, built to restrain the incursions of the Tartars. This structure is about 1500 English miles in length; has a height of 27 feet; its thickness at top is 14 feet. The lower portion of it is built of dressed stone, the upper of well burned brick. It is flanked at distances of about 80 yards apart by towers in which iron cannon are found.

In the great extent it embraces, it necessarily crosses hills and valleys, and in many places important defiles. An examination of its parts has shown that in its plan there was an evident design to adapt it to those features of its site, as it is well thrown back to the rear of difficult passes; and at points where there is most danger to be apprehended from attempts of invasion, there are several walls in succession.

**275.** The mode of attack of fortified places resorted to by the ancients was reduced to settled rules, and brought to the highest state of perfection by the Greeks, about the epoch of Alexander the Great and the immediate successors to his vast conquests. An essential feature in it, whether in the sieges of inland fortresses or those on the seaboard, was to cut off all communication between the place and the exterior, by hemming it in by sea and land, with stationary forces, covered themselves by lines of intrenchments strengthened by towers, and, in the case of sea-coast places, also by fleets, from all assaults both from without and from the place invested.

Having selected the portions of the place on which the attack was to be directed, a second line was formed parallel to the first, which was covered, and constructed of timber and wicker-work, and secured with raw hides to prevent its being set on fire. From this sheltered position, which served also the purposes of a lodging for the besiegers, the besieged were annoyed with missiles thrown from all the artillery known in that day, consisting of the ordinary bow, the cross-bow, and the various machines for projecting heavy stones and other projectiles.

Under the diversion thus made, the besiegers pushed forward from this line several covered approaches of a like construction directly upon the place, for the purpose of gaining the counterscarp of the place, and from that position filling up the ditch with stones, earth, heavy logs, &c., to prepare the way for placing the battering-ram in position to breach the wall. The tower in which this machine was placed usually consisted of several stories, and was occupied by troops who cleared the top of the wall assailed of the besieged. This operation was frequently aided by other high towers, which were advanced either along the natural level of the ground, or upon artificial mounds forming inclined planes, towards the place, by means of which the towers could be given any desirable command over the interior.

**276.** The defence was mostly of a passive character; the besiegers trusting mainly to the strength of their defences, under cover of which they resorted to all the means used by the besiegers, for attaining the latter when they came within reach of their missiles; using cranes and other devices to seize upon the implements planted at the foot of the wall, and carrying out galleries of countermines to overwhelm the artificial mounds and their towers.

**277.** The Romans evinced their decided military aptitude, not only in the employment of the ordinary systematic methods of the attack and defence of fortified places, but in their application of the cardinal principle of mutual defensive relations between the parts of a fortified position, obtained by advanced and retired portions of the enceinte; and also in the adaptation of intrenchments to the natural features of the site, as shown in the fortifications of some of the permanent frontier camps of their military colonies. These principles have also been noticed in some of the fortified positions of India, which consist of a mural enceinte with the earthen ramparts flanked by round towers, and of round towers in advance of the enceinte connected with it by caponnières.

With the decadence of the Roman Empire, the art of fortification, like the other branches of the military art, was brought to so low a stage that strongholds which, skilfully defended with energy, would have baffled the efforts of a well-trained assailant in the art of attack, fell, almost without resistance, into the possession of the fierce northern hordes, by which the whole of civilized Europe was overrun.

**278.** The remains of the structures raised for defensive purposes, during the prosperous days of the Empire, were probably the sole means of protection afforded to the inhabitants of the towns that still maintained a nucleus of population, until the rise of the Western Empire, under Charlemagne; and it was the necessity felt by this conqueror, not only of securing his conquests, but of checking the irruptions of the barbarous tribes along his extended frontier, which led him to erect *têtes-de-pont* on the frontier rivers, and a line of strong towers, for garrisons of a few men, upon the most inaccessible and prominent points of this frontier; the latter being a means which was subsequently resorted to for a like purpose in the Spanish peninsula.

Henry I., of Germany, introduced a more important and more systematic addition to these permanent frontier defences, by surrounding the frontier towns and villages, occupied by military colonists, with walls and ditches, to secure them from such attacks as they might be exposed to, and subsequently adding a second line of strongholds within the frontier, by which an irruption through the frontier line might still be checked.

**279.** During the general disorganization of states under the feudal system, the free cities, which depended for their defence on the burghers composing the different crafts, every individual who could maintain a few retainers in his pay, and the clergy, even, resorted—each according to their separate views—to such means of defence as would best secure them from the attacks of others in a like condition, and would enable them to carry out that system of pillage which had become general amongst the nobles and other military chieftains.

**280.** From this state of society sprung up those castles, placed in the most inaccessible positions on the lines of communication which the little inland commerce that was still carried on was obliged to traverse. These were provided with every possible device for an obstinate passive defence, being surrounded by a wide and deep ditch, or moat, over which a drawbridge was the only communication to the main entrance, which was flanked by towers on the exterior, and closed with massive doors; the tortuous passage which led from them to the interior of the castle being further secured by a grated portcullis, which could be let drop at a moment's notice, to arrest a sudden assault.

To these means were often joined, besides the ordinary measures of loop-holes and machicoulis in the walls and towers for annoying the assailant, a high interior tower, termed a keep, or donjon, which, commanding the exterior defences, was also a watch-tower over the adjacent country.

The keep, which was the last defensible point, was, in some cases, provided with a secret subterranean passage, having its outlet in some distant concealed spot, through which succor could be introduced into the beleaguered castle; and, in the last extremity, the garrison find safety in a stealthy flight.

**281.** The fortifications of towns partook of the same characteristics as those of castles. From the custom of assigning to the different burgher crafts, each of which had an independent military organization, the exclusive guardianship of portions of the enceinte, as well as their erection and repairs, great diversity, and frequently a whimsicality, in the defensive arrangements was the natural result; the evidence of which still exists in the remains of the walls of some of the old Continental cities. The art, for the most part, was practised by ambulatory engineers, who, like the secret orders by whom the bridges and churches of the same period were built, offered their services wherever they were wanted. Many ideas were also introduced from the East by the Crusaders, as exhibited in the fortifications of castles and cities belonging to the Templars and other religious military orders.

**282.** With the invention of gunpowder, and its application to military purposes, a gradual revolution took place in the general forms and details of fortification. It was soon seen that naked walls alone did not offer either suitable conveniences for the new military machines, or sufficient protection against the projectiles thrown from them. This led to the introduction of earthen ramparts and parapets, which were placed against the walls and suitably arranged to meet the exigencies of the moment. The art received something like a scientific basis about this time, in Italy, from which the names and forms of most of the elements of fortification now in use are derived. The Italian engineers, like their predecessors, went from state to state to offer their services wherever they were needed, and in this way disseminated the principles of their school throughout Europe.

**283.** It was at this epoch that the bastioned form of fortification first appeared, but the precise date and the author of the invention are both unknown. With its introduction the importance of separating the parts of a line of fortification into advanced and retired parts, the latter flanking and defending the former, seems to have been recognised as an essential principle of the art. With these changes in the form of the enceinte, the art was gradually improved by the addition of outworks to increase the amount of cross and flank fire; the introduction of bomb-proof shelters for the troops and other purposes; the substitution of earthen for stone parapets; and the attempt to conceal the scarp walls from the enemy's batteries by decreasing the command and deepening the ditches of the enceinte.

By these gradual changes stone walls, which in the old fortifications were the essential defensive features, came at length to be regarded in their true character, simply as passive obstacles to an open assault by escalade. The property of earthen parapets, of resisting without material loss of strength the long-continued fire of the assailant's heaviest guns, showed that the same defensive means were applicable both to works of a permanent and of a temporary character; and were equally available for the purposes of the assailant and the assailed. The measures for the attack and the defence of positions were thus reduced to the same general principles, differing only in the forms and dimensions of the elementary parts, as circumstances seemed to demand.

**284. Italian School.** As above stated, the first employment of bastions as they now exist was made by the Italian engineers; and, as far as has been ascertained, towards the close of the fifteenth or the commencement of the sixteenth century. To whom the credit of their invention is due is not known. In the earlier fronts of the Italian school the bastions are very small, and they are connected by curtains varying from 250 to 500 yards in length. The bastion flanks, which were perpendicular to the curtains, were divided into two portions; that next to the curtain, which was one-third of the entire flank, was thrown back and covered by the portion in advance, which thus formed what received the name of the orillon. The lower part of the retired portion was casemated for cannon; and behind this, and separated from it by a dry ditch, rose a second flank, having the same command as the other parts of the enceinte parapet. In some cases a small and very obtuse bastion was erected at the middle of long curtains.

The ditches of the enceinte were usually about 100 feet wide and 24 feet deep; the counterscarps being parallel to the bastion-faces.

A scarp gallery, for the purpose of mining, ran throughout the enceinte scarp, and communicated with galleries leading to other points.

The parapets, at first of masonry, were afterwards of earth, and from 18 to 24 feet thick. The earth of the rampart was sustained on the interior by a wall. Ramps established a communication between the interior and the rampart.

The defects of these early fronts were soon felt, and a more complicated but improved method adopted, in which the bastions were enlarged and the curtains diminished. The retired flanks were still retained, but the orillon instead of being angular was rounded. To these improvements, cavaliers were sometimes added to the bastions, which in those cases were made without retired flanks; or placed on the curtains, when, from the configuration of the site, some portion of the ground within cannon-range could not be swept from the enceinte parapet. The covered-way was introduced and became an integral part of the front; and a small demi-lune or ravelin was placed in advance of the enceinte ditch, forming a *tête-de-pont* to cover the communication, at the middle of the curtain across the main ditch, between the enceinte and the exterior. The covered-way, which at first was of uniform width and bordered the main and demi-lune ditches, was subsequently provided with salient and reëntering places-of-arms. These various essential parts of a fortified front were gradually ameliorated by the Italian engineers, but not before the Italian school had left its impress upon the fortification of all the other states of Europe; as the Italian engineers, from their superior acquirements, were in demand throughout these states.

**285. Spanish School.** From the existing fortifications of Spain, the influence of the Italian school may be traced, but modified by national characteristics; the works seem organized more for a purely passive defence; the covered-way, that essential outwork to an active defence, being in many cases omitted; the means of annoying the besiegers by fires being greatly multiplied; and the outworks generally being arranged with a view to a purely passive defence. Besides this, the dimensions of the profile and height of scarp were increased as a greater security against escalade; interior retrenchments were multiplied, sometimes enclosing a bomb-proof keep to render the defence more obstinate.

The Spaniards, although resorting but little to sorties show great skill and pertinacity in the defence of breaches, and in availing themselves of all obstructions for prolonging resistance.

From the broken character of many of the sites of their fortresses, the Spaniards resorted very much also to detached works to occupy commanding points from which the main work could be annoyed.

These they also generally organized for a strictly passive defence, leaving them more to their own resources than to any coöperation with the main work.

**286. Dutch School.** This school took its rise in the political necessities of the times, in which the national spirit was aroused to throw off an onerous foreign yoke. The aquatic character of the country, and the want of time and pecuniary means, led to those expedients of defence which are never wanting under like circumstances. The deficiency of earth led to the formation of low parapets for the main enceinte and wide ditches filled with water. The main enceinte was usually preceded by a second one with a very low parapet to sweep the surface of the wet ditch; and this second enceinte was separated from the first by a dry ditch, which favored sorties, and which was provided with all the means, as palisades, tambours, and block-houses, for offensive returns and surprises. The second enceinte was generally covered from an exterior command by a glacis in advance of the main ditch. The covered-way between the glacis and the ditches was, to a great extent, deprived of its essential offensive feature by an exterior wet ditch, made at the foot of the glacis and enclosing it, over which communication with the exterior was kept open by temporary bridges.

The works were usually very much multiplied and their combination complicated; features the less objectionable where their defence chiefly rested upon the inhabitants who had become familiar with all their turnings, and as offering obscurity of design to an assailant who might force his way into them. The whole of the defensive measures of this school seem to have had solely for their object a strictly passive resistance. With this view long lines of intrenchments, supported from distance to distance by forts, connected their frontier towns and villages, affording a sufficient obstacle to marauding expeditions, and requiring the efforts of a strong force to break through them. At a later period, taught by the experience of their earlier efforts against the most military state of that epoch, covers that would afford security against incendiary modes of attack were provided; and revetments of masonry substituted for the earthen slopes of the ramparts, particularly where the ditches were dry. These successive changes, partly influenced by the Italian and Spanish schools, with which the

Dutch engineers were brought into contact through their connection with Spain, were the natural precursors of the system of Coehoorn, the most distinguished engineer of the Dutch school, whose works are characterized by many of its essential features.

**287. German School.** The Germans reckon a number of original writers on fortification, among the most noted of whom are the celebrated painter, Albert Durer, Daniel Speckles, and Rimpler. In the propositions of these writers are to be found the influence which the Italian school naturally exercised throughout civilized Europe, and the germs of many of the views held by the German school of the present day; which last seem, however, to have been taken more immediately from the propositions of Montalembert and Carnot.

**288. Swedish School.** The part played by Sweden upon the theatre of Europe, under her two celebrated monarchs, Gustavus Adolphus and Charles XII., served to develop in this nation every branch of the military art, and produced a number of distinguished generals and engineers, who combined with the practice of their profession, a study of its theory. Among the engineers of this school, Virgin holds the first place.

The climate and the nautical habits of the country seem to have led to land defences analogous to those of ships, as shown in the uses of casemated batteries in several tiers, both for sea-coast and inland fortifications. In this school the bastioned system seems to have been generally adopted for the enceinte, great attention being paid to covering the faces of the works from enfilading fire; in providing casemates having reverse views on the besiegers' works; and particularly in so arranging the interior dispositions that each part should not only contribute to the defence of the others, but be capable of an independent resistance. These dispositions necessarily led to great complication and multiplicity of works, as shown in the writings of Virgin.

**289. French School.** What may be termed the characteristics of this school are to be seen rather in the method of Cormontaingne, and the teachings of the two celebrated schools of Mézières and Metz for the education of engineers, than in the practice of Vauban, although his authority has exercised a preponderating influence throughout Europe, and is still appealed to, in all great problems of the art, by each side in polemical disputes.

The French have evinced in this, as in all the other arts,

that spirit of systematic combination which forms one of their most striking national traits. Without excluding an active defence, the most noted authors of this school have based their methods more upon a combination of elements by which the besieger's progress can be checked step by step by the fire of the works than by sorties. Until within the last thirty or forty years the French school was perhaps open to the reproach of a too exclusive method, and a subjection to mere authority. This accusation, however, was true rather of the polemical writings of the present day, growing out of the propositions of Montalembert, than of the practice of the French engineers; and it was in a measure strengthened by a misconception of the real purposes of the instruction given in their schools of professional training. Still recognising in Vauban and Cormontaingne the chief founders and authorities of their school, the French engineers of the present day discard no defensive element that has stood the test of experience, or is consonant with sound professional views; basing their art upon incontrovertible principles, its practice is made by them to conform to the exigencies of each case as presented by its own data.

## II.

### PROGRESS OF THE ATTACK SINCE THE INVENTION OF FIRE-ARMS.

**290.** The introduction of cannon, although it led to important changes in the measures both of the attack and defence, still did not, for a considerable period, bring about any very decisive results in the length of sieges. The means which it afforded the defence of reaching the besiegers at a distance, and of destroying all the methods of approaching and annoying the place which had been hitherto used, led to the substitution of the ordinary trenches of the present day for the wooden galleries and other similar expedients for approaching under cover, and to the erection of batteries at distant points to open breaches in the walls.

Lines of circumvallation and countervallation, which formed so prominent a feature previously to this epoch, was the only one which still kept its place, as it has done to a greater or less extent to the present day. For the purpose of effecting an entrance into the place, breaching batteries were erected opposite the points deemed most favorable.

They were placed either on natural elevations of the ground, or upon artificial mounds, with the object of attaining the wall to be opened near its foot, and to form a breach of easy ascent. These batteries were enclosed in works of sufficient size and strength to hold garrisons to secure them from sorties. The approaches were made as at present, by zigzags along the capitals of the salients to the counterscarp, where a covered descent was made into the ditch opposite the breach preparatory to its assault. When the wall was not exposed to a distant fire, the besiegers were obliged to carry the covered-way by assault, and establish their breaching batteries on the crest of the glacis.

In carrying forward these works the besiegers were subjected to great losses and delays, owing to the magnitude and multiplicity of the works they were obliged to complete; to the imperfect character of their artillery and the faulty position of their batteries, by which they were unable to keep under the fire of the place; the want of connection between the separate approaches, and the consequent exposure of the workmen in the trenches to sorties, the troops for their support being too distant in the enclosed works in the rear to give them timely succor; besides which, as these enclosed works naturally became the chief objects for the fire of the besieged, this agglomeration of troops in them added materially to the losses of the besiegers.

Owing to these imperfections in the measures of attack, the besieged were able to make a vigorous and prolonged defence; and sieges became the most important military operations of this period, in which captains of the greatest celebrity sought for opportunities of distinction.

**291.** But little deviation was made in the methods just described until Vauban appeared upon the scene. Previously to him, Montluc, a distinguished French general and engineer of his day, had introduced short branches of trenches, which were run out from the angles of the zigzags, to post a few troops for the immediate protection of the workmen; but these were found to be very insufficient in repelling sorties of any strength.

The event which seems to have had the greatest influence on the subsequent progress of both the attack and defence was the memorable siege of Candia, in which volunteers from all parts of Europe engaged, and who, after its close, disseminated throughout their respective countries the results of the experience they had there acquired.

Whether the idea of the parallels, now in use in the attack, originated there, or with Vauban, this eminent man was the first to establish them in a systematic manner, and to demonstrate by experience their controlling importance in repressing sorties. The introduction of this important element in the attack; the concentration of the fire of batteries, by giving them enfilading positions; the invention of the ricochet, as the most powerful destructive means against the defences; the avoidance of open assaults, which, even when successful, are made at a great sacrifice of life, preferring to them the less brilliant but slower method of skill and industry, by which the blood of the soldier is spared, and the end more surely attained, such are the important services which the attack owes to Vauban, which has given it its present marked superiority over the means of defence, and to which the science and experience of engineers since his day have added nothing of marked importance.

**292. Remarks.** Whilst the attack has thus been brought to such a state of perfection, and its destructive means are still on the increase, from the rapid improvement daily making in the range and certainty of aim of cannon, the means of defence, so far as relates to fortifications alone, are but little if at all in advance of what they were in the time of Vauban.

Upon the chief defects and wants of the art there exists but slight divergence of opinion among engineers generally; not so with respect to the remedy; opposite opinions being frequently drawn from the same class of facts, and the same authority being frequently cited to sustain opposite views. Whilst each new disputant denounces systematizing and the systems of others, his remedy for the abuse complained of is usually a system of his own, which not unfrequently is but a combination of the *disjecta membra* of those of others.

The sum of the whole matter is, that fortification is an art the component elements and principles of which are few and simple. Its efficiency consists neither in short lines of defence nor long lines of defence; neither in large nor small bastions, nor in the adoption of this or that system; but in the judicious adaptation of these principles and elements to the locality to be defended, and the purposes of the defence. In this resides the excellence of the engineer's art. He who should combine his elements in the arrangement of a small work with a weak garrison as he would in one intended for the occupation of an extensive position by a large force, or should blindly adopt the same methods for an irregular site that he would for a horizontal one, whatever his acquisitions or pretensions may be, has but a small claim to the title of military engineer.

From the preceding brief summary, it will be seen that the art of fortification, in its progress, has kept pace with the measures of the attack; its successive changes having been brought about by changes either in the arms used by the assailant, or by the introduction of some new mode of assault. The same causes must continue to produce the same effects. At no past period has mechanical invention, in its bearing on the military art, been more active than at the present day. The improvement that has already been made in the range and accuracy of aim of both small-arms and cannon, the partial adoption of wrought-iron and steel for floating batteries and sea-coast defences, point to the commencement of another epoch in the engineer's art. The great improvement in cannon will give to the assailant a still wider range in the selection of positions for his batteries, and will thus increase the difficulties of the engineer in adapting his works to the site, and in giving adequate shelter to the garrison and armanent. Whilst the defence will be to this extent weakened, the approaches of the besieger will be rendered more perilous and more difficult from the greater range and accuracy of small-arms.

The great destruction of life in open assaults by columns, exposed within so long a range, must give an additional value to intrenched fields of battle; and we may again see field-works play the part they did in the defence of Sebastopol, and positions so chosen and fortified, that not only will the assailant be forced to intrench himself to assail them, but will find the varying phases of his attack met by corresponding changes in the defensive dispositions.

**293.** In our own country, from the circumstances of our position, permanent fortification has met with its most frequent applications in works planned for sea-coast defence, in which our engineers, without servilely copying any of the systems in vogue in Europe, have followed the bastioned system, wherever the works were of such an extent as to admit of its application.

In the larger works erected by them for sea-coast defence, the water-fronts consist of one or more tiers of casemated batteries, surmounted by one in barbette, whilst the land fronts consist of the usual rampart and parapet arranged for open defences.

In the smaller works, which, from the limited extent of their fronts, did not admit of the adoption of the bastioned system, flanking dispositions have been made, either by casemated caponnières or counterscarp galleries.

Wherever the site was very limited, and a large amount of fire in a given direction was desirable, as in the cases of islands (either natural or artificial) to be occupied on the line of a channel to a roadstead or harbor, the castellated form, consisting of several tiers of casemates, surmounted by a barbette battery, has been adopted. These works are generally so surrounded by water as to be secure from an open assault, and therefore not requiring flanking dispositions. Wherever, however, it has been thought necessary to place these, small bastioned towers have been added at the salient angles of the work.

Whilst thus adhering to well-settled principles, and following the practice of the best European authorities, our engineers have contributed their share to the improvement of the details of the art. The works erected by them within the last half-century are remarkable for the excellence of the materials employed, the great skill shown in their construction, and the care with which every detail was worked out to subserve the object in view. In these respects—in the inventive genius often displayed—and in the adaptation of the plan to the site, it is not claiming too much to say that the works erected by them are not surpassed, and in some points not equalled, by any similar works in Europe.

As to what future changes will be called for in permanent fortifications, both for inland and sea-coast defence, time alone can develop. Judging from the increasing size and range of cannon, and their greater destructive effects, it is probable that wrought-iron will have to be substituted for stone in positions where the latter is exposed to the heavy projectiles coming into use, as this material and earthen parapets will alone afford an indestructible cover against such projectiles. Still, when we look to the time and care which are given to the erection of permanent works, the great superiority they have over temporary structures for the planting and handling the heaviest cannon, besides the difficulty which the transportation of such enormous weapons offers to their use by the assailant, there is no reason why these changes should not inure to the advantage of the defence, both on land and water fronts.

In the defence of harbors and rivers against the most imposing means of attack by heavily-armed iron-clad steamers, there is every reason to suppose that an adequate means will be found, in floating and stationary obstructions, like booms and torpedoes, combined with iron-clad floating batteries, to secure them from all hazard.

Plate 3.

Fig. 1
A
B
C
D
Fig. 2
Profile on A B.
Horizontal
Fig. 3
Elevation on C D.
Horizontal
Fig. 4
Line of Natural Ground
A
B
C
D
H
Fig. 5
X
Y
Z
Fig. 6
E
F
G
Fig. 7
Fig. 8
E
A
Fig. 9
A
B
C
D
E
Fig. 10
A
B
C
D
E
Fig. 11
A
B
C
D
E
Fig. 12
Fig. 13

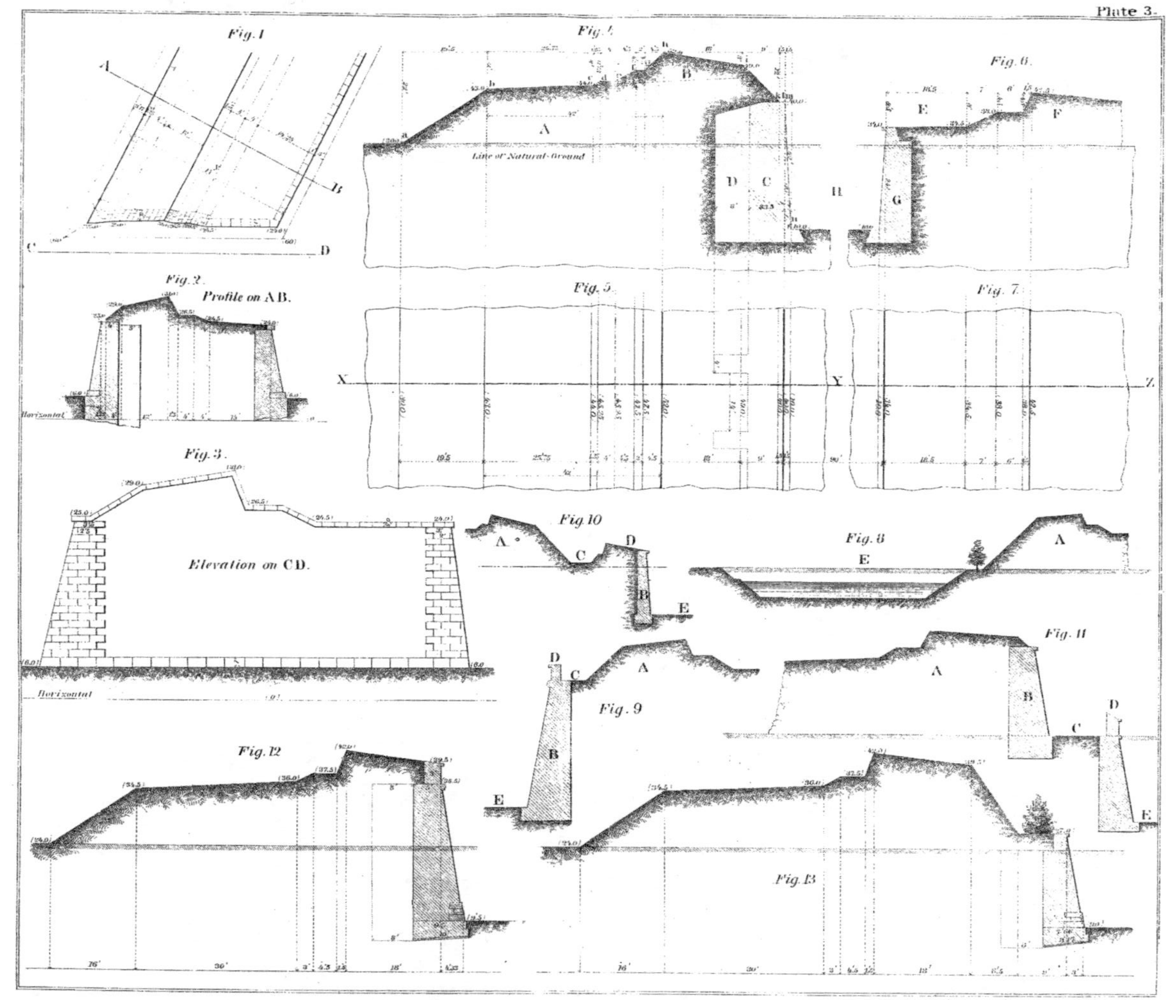

Plate 4.

Fig. 14.
Fig. 15.
Fig. 16.
Fig. 17.
Fig. 18.
Fig. 19.
Fig. 20.
Fig. 21.
Fig. 22.
Fig. 23.
Fig. 24.
Fig. 25.
Fig. 26.
Fig. 27.
Fig. 28.
Fig. 28.
Fig. 30.
Fig. 31.
Fig. 32.
Fig. 33
Fig. 34.
Fig. 35

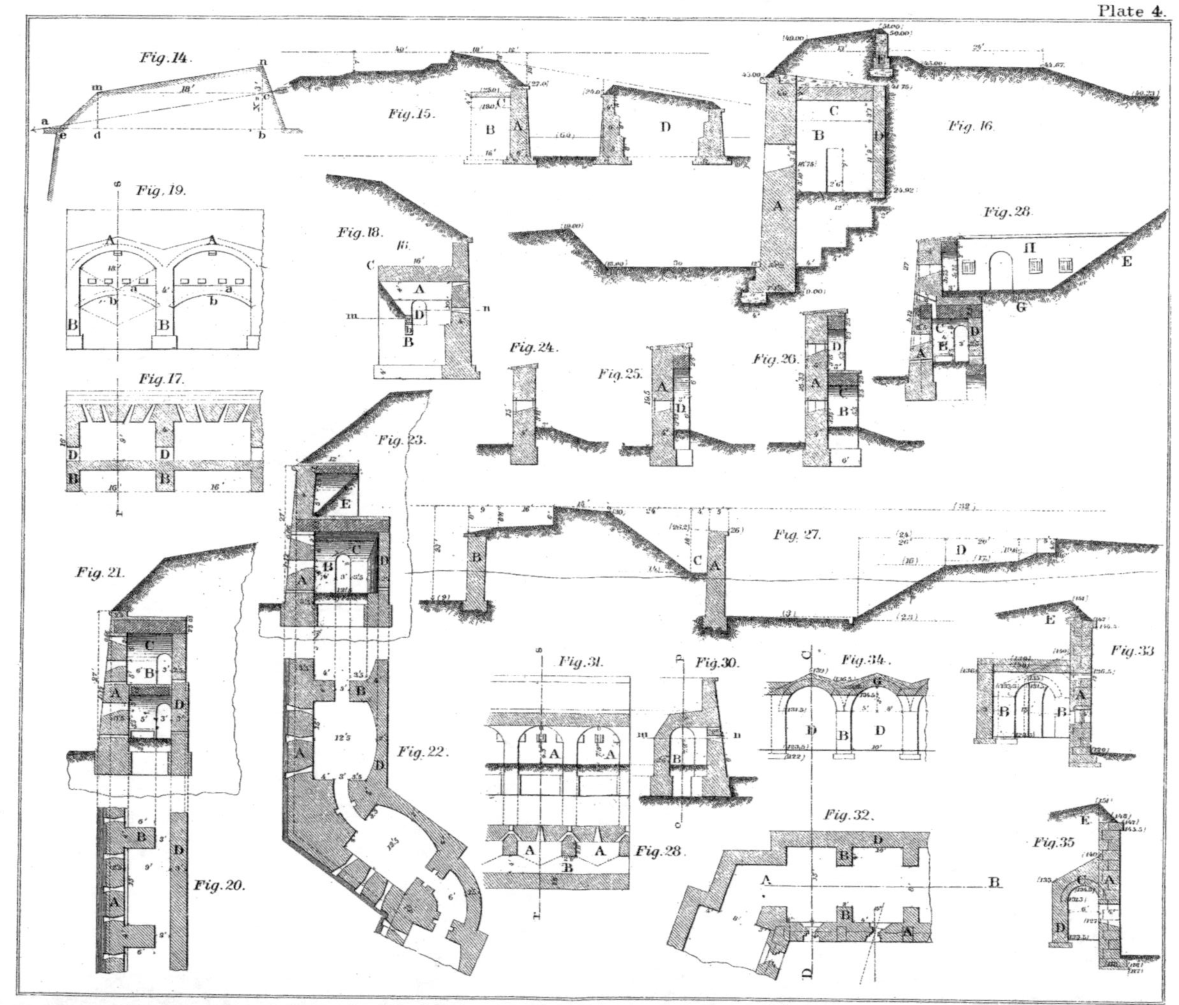

Plate 5.

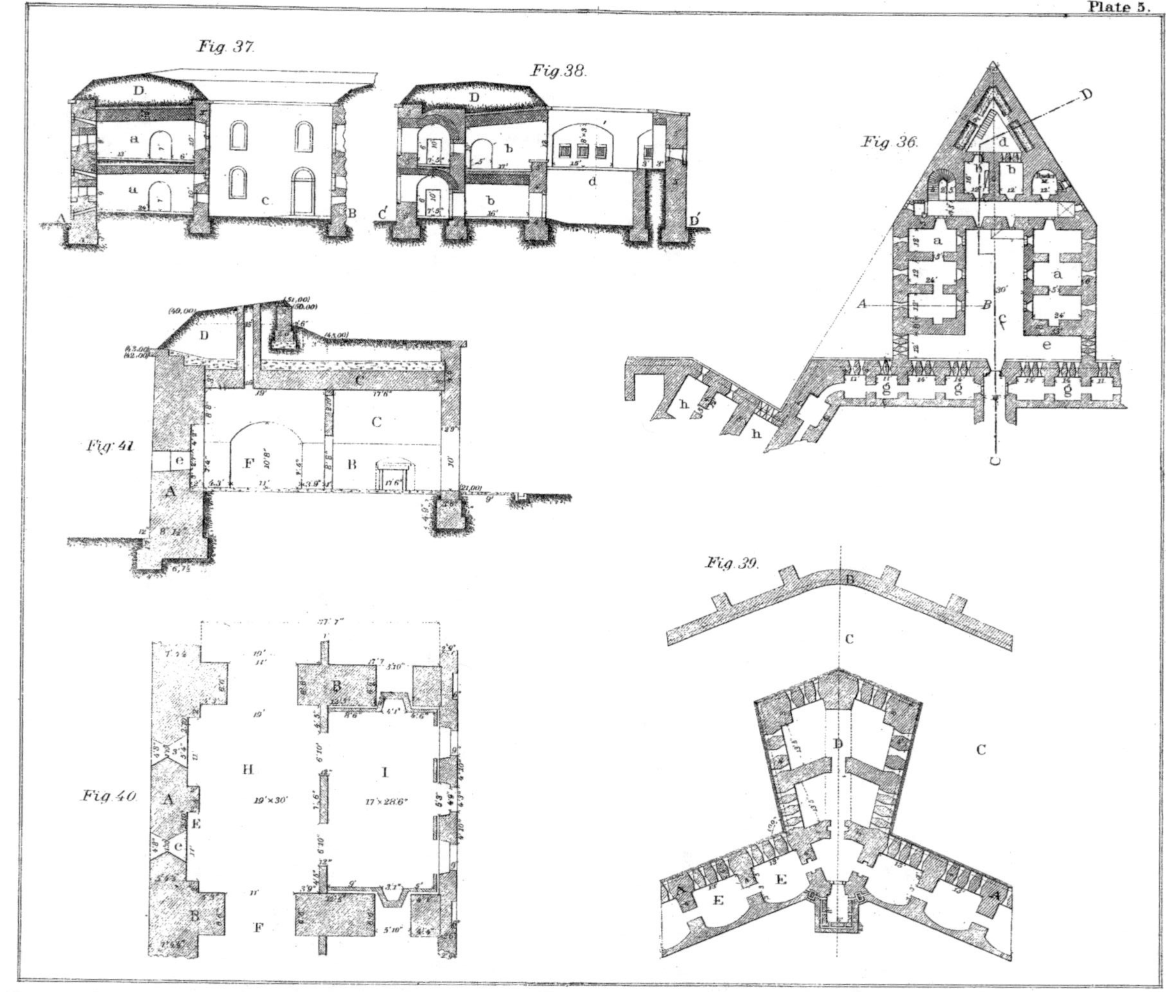

Plate 6.

Fig. 42.
Fig. 43.
Fig. 44.
Fig. 45.
Fig. 46.
Fig. 47.
Fig. 48.
Fig. 49.
Fig. 50.
High Water
Low Water

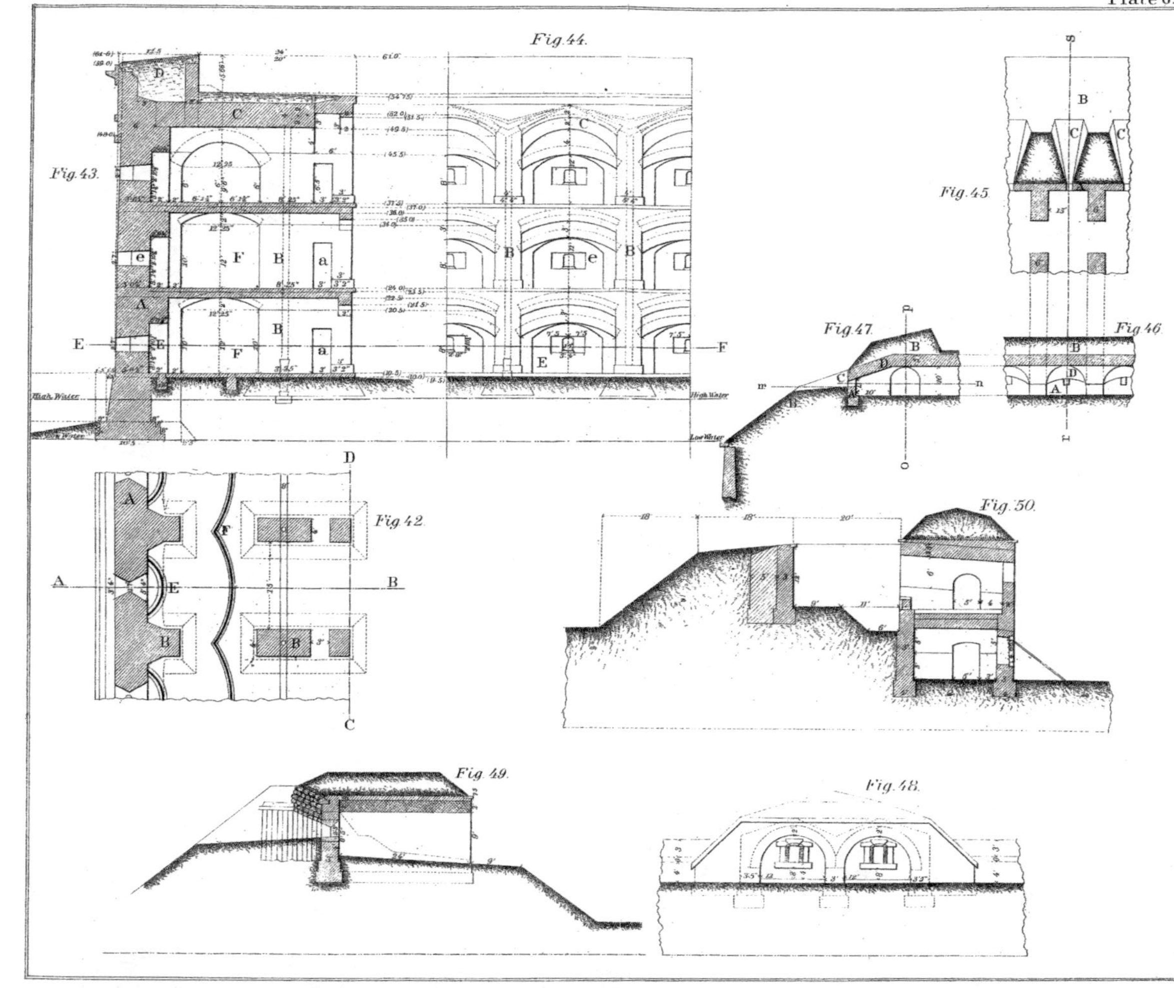

Plate 7.

Fig. 54.
Fig. 55.
Fig. 56.
Fig. 57.
Fig. 52.
Fig. 58.
Fig. 51.
Fig. 53.
Fig. 60.
Fig. 59.
A
B
D

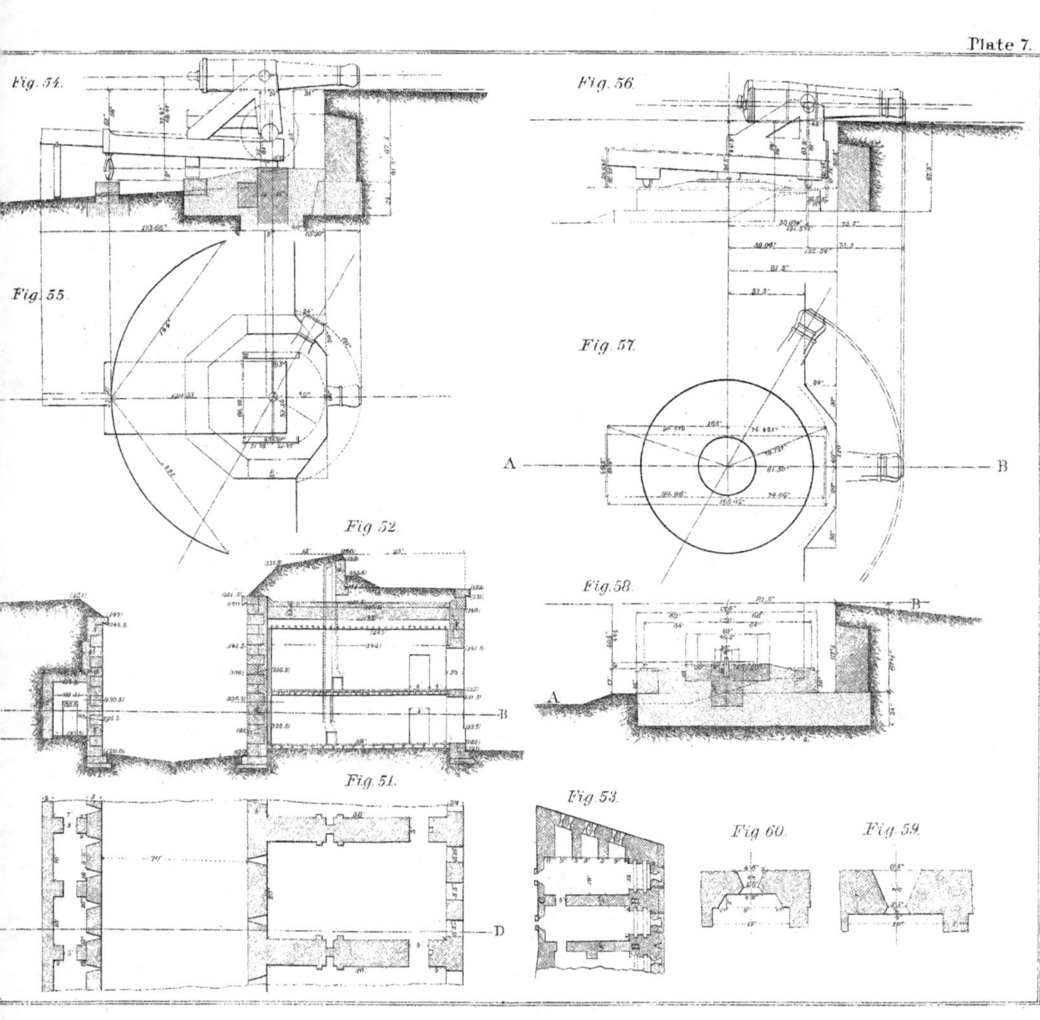

Plate 8.

Fig. 65.
Fig. 66.
Fig. 64
Fig. 63.
Fig. 62
Fig. 68.
Fig. 67
Fig. 70
Fig. 71
Fig. 61
Fig. 76.
Fig. 69
Fig. 78
Fig. 77.
Fig. 80
Fig. 79
Fig. 72.
Fig. 75
Fig. 74
Fig. 73.

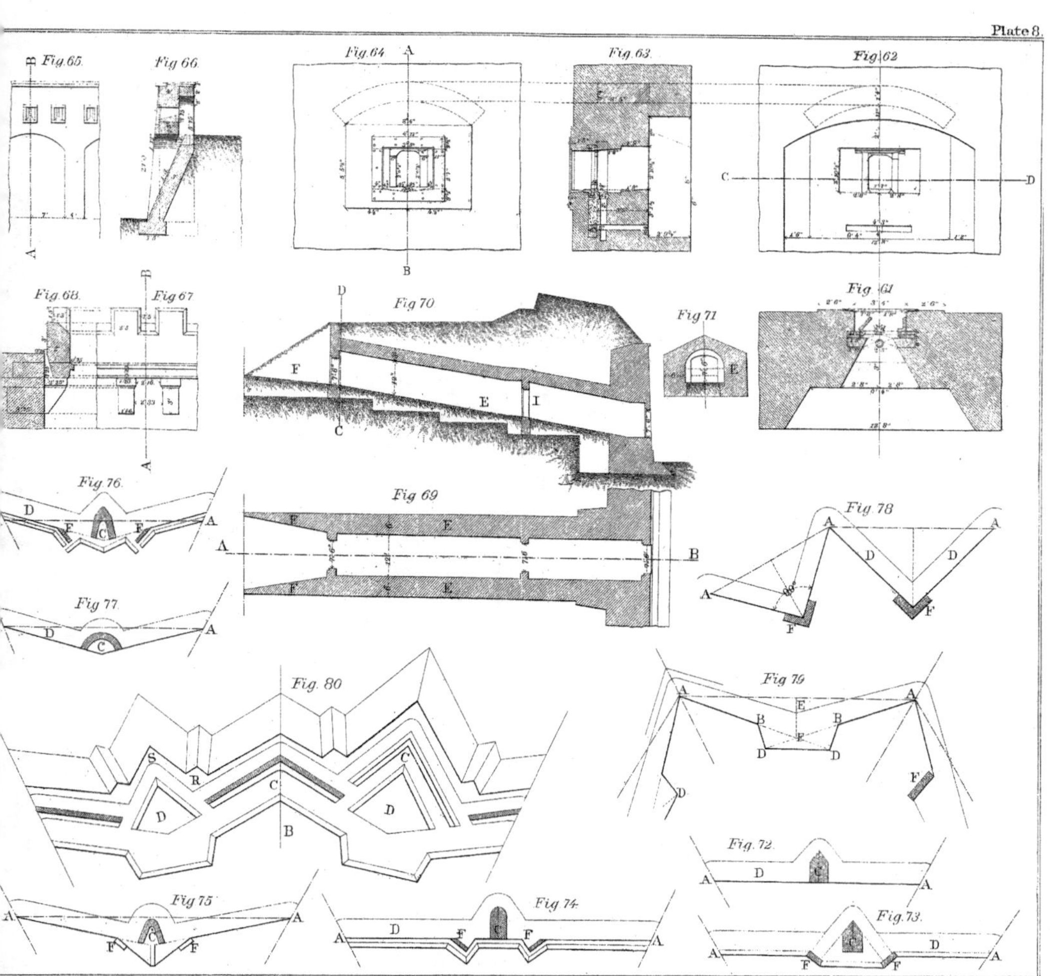

Plate 9.

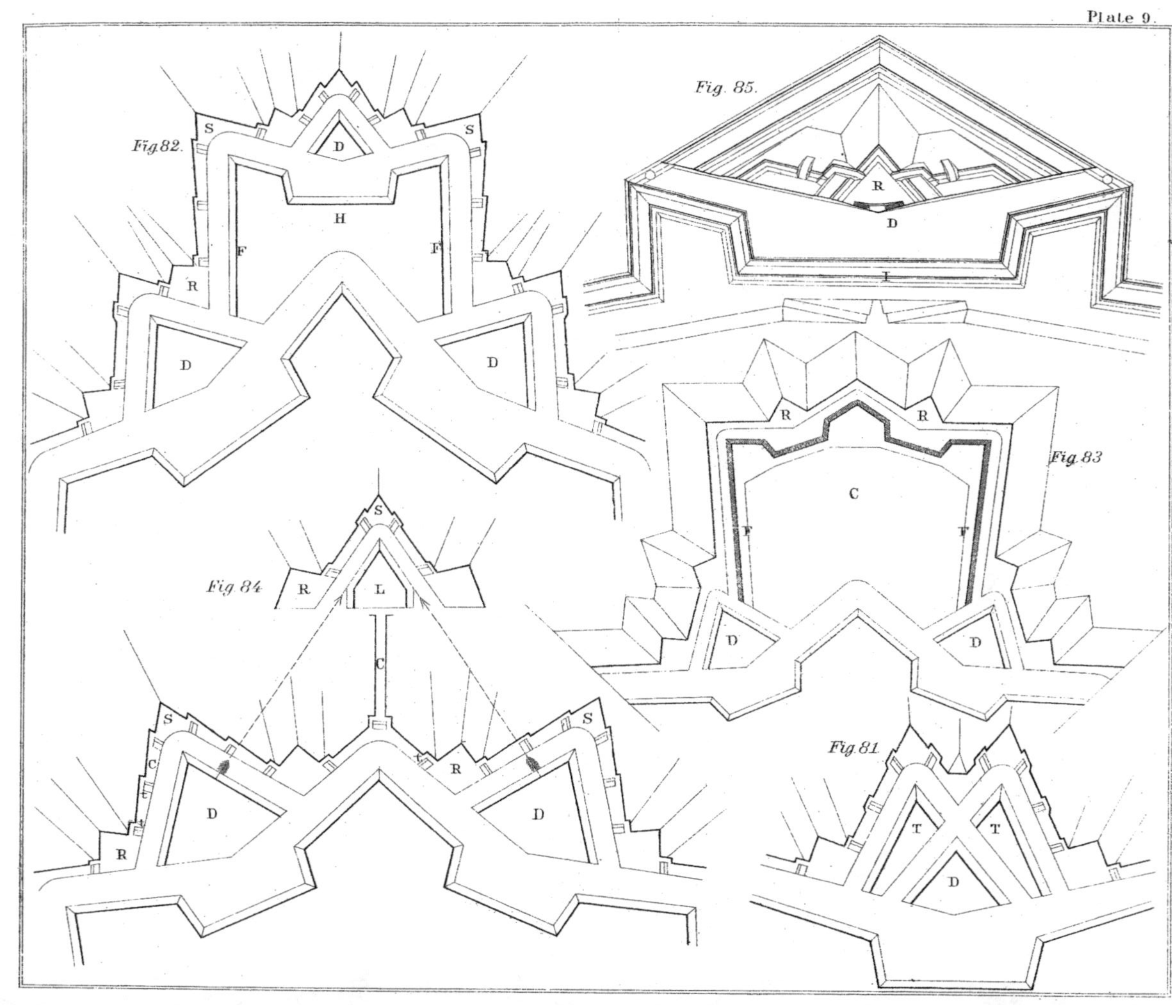

www.ingramcontent.com/pod-product-compliance
Lightning Source LLC
LaVergne TN
LVHW011221110826
845150LV00006B/1496

* 9 7 8 1 4 2 5 5 1 6 1 6 1 *